SAVING STORMIE

—— THE BABY **S** STORY ——

Crystal Kelley and **Elisabeth Collins**

ISBN-10 1523959207
ISBN-13 978-1523959204

'Saving Stormie: The Baby S Story' is published by Crystal Kelley and Elisabeth Collins. Elisabeth can be contacted at:

www.elisabethcollins.com
www.facebook.com/elisabethcollinsauthor

Based on a true story.

> You will never do anything in this world without courage.
>
> It is the greatest quality of the mind next to honor.
>
> —Aristotle

CHAPTER ONE
June 24, 2012

There was one thing I was sure of, Stormie—you were going to be born today.

   After the first attempt at induction failed a few days earlier, both you and I were finally ready to meet each other. For months doctors had told us you would be different, but I saw the diagnosis as beautiful and unique, not challenging.

   The nurses had asked me to arrive at the hospital on Sunday in the early evening and I was there on time. Scott and I decided to walk the nine blocks from my apartment to the hospital and I was thankful for the cool, breezy night. Michigan could get very hot and humid in the summer and I was glad I didn't have to bear the sweltering heat of August while pregnant. I was still feeling good, and paused in front of the hospital doors for one last glance at my pregnant body. Luckily the past nine months had served me well and most of my weight gain had been in my belly. People said that from behind you couldn't even tell I was pregnant.

I looked at Scott. "Well, this is it. No turning back now," I said, and walked through the entrance.

After checking in, a nurse took Scott and me to our room. As we were led down a long sterile hallway, Scott held my hand and glanced over at me. Our eyes met and he smiled, the same smile that had come across his face when I had my first two babies. He squinted and tilted his head, letting me know he was by my side for support. Today we were bringing you into the world, Stormie. As a couple we'd had our challenges but together we had endured almost a year of provocation in the greatest controversy of our lives. We stood firm and fought back, and if not for a whirlwind of trial and tribulation, you may never have been born.

■　■　■

The room was large and smelled like fresh orange cleaner, not the medicinal scent I had expected. I specifically requested the labor room with a large tub, knowing the water would help relieve some of the pressure during contractions. After all, I had done this twice already and this time I had made specific plans so I could be as relaxed as possible. However, the nurses told me that I wouldn't be in this room during delivery; the medical staff wanted to move me to an operating room where a team of neonatal experts could be ready for any less than ideal outcome that might occur. They weren't sure you could take your first breath without medical intervention and needed all hands on deck when you were born.

So really, there were two things I was sure of—that you would be born today and that your birth wouldn't be anything like anyone expected. A pregnant woman could plan and prepare but when the time came to actually give birth, it was the baby's decision about how the laboring hours would go.

Scott and I got the room set up, placing colorful index cards near me with inspirational phrases like 'breathe' and 'trust your body.' I laid a string of birthing beads I had received on top of some of the cards. Each member of my mom's group, as well as several other friends, had given me a bead to serve as a reminder of the support I had in doing the right thing for you. My diffuser was loaded with tranquility essential oils, and peaceful music flowed from an app on my phone—music I knew you would love too, Stormie. A pleasant environment was important if I was to get through this without using pain medication, which could be so detrimental to you.

In my mind, I had to do everything I could to make sure you had the best start to whatever your life would bring. Throughout the pregnancy, as difficult as it was emotionally, I stood firm in my belief that life was precious and you deserved to be born. It terrified me to have no idea about what was to come, but I knew that your little life inside my belly deserved at least a fighting chance.

I wanted to do everything in my power to have you naturally but Pitocin was a necessity in order to move things along. I was dreading it, as I'd had Pitocin in my first birth, but the days of prodromal labor were wearing me down. The use of Pitocin meant that my contractions would be longer, more intense, and much closer together, but as my family had arrived a few days earlier and would be leaving shortly, the sooner I could have you the better.

Within the hour after receiving the IV, I could feel the intensity of the contractions tightening my stomach and leaving me short of breath, but the calming words I had written on my arms quickly brought me to a tranquil state. One forearm held the word 'Release', while the other displayed 'Peace.' They served as a constant reminder that I could do this naturally by remaining calm. This method, known as Hypnobabies, taught me to stay in a state of relaxation throughout labor.

Soon my mother arrived. "Looks like you're having a day at the spa," she said.

Scott and I laughed, dispersing the nervousness we were feeling. Maybe I should have been fearful of the upcoming pain I would experience but I was confident in my body and focused on keeping you safe. I would work through the cramping and intensity of birth because the months leading up to this point had been more torture than I would ever experience physically.

With my contractions getting closer and closer together, I knew it was time to call the photographer and the doula who had volunteered their time for this day. Ashley, my photographer, arrived first and began taking snapshots of the minutes that would soon become memories. Thankfully, she was also a doula and helped me in the first stages of labor when the bed no longer served as a comfortable place to rest my distressed body. We tried a few positions but none of them relieved the pressure. Finally the peanut ball on the floor, with me leaning over it, became my solace. It held me up until my legs could no longer support my weight. Kristin, my doula, came just as I had decided it was time to get into the tub.

As I undressed, I thought about how the protective shield of my body only served to safeguard you physically. I wanted you to be protected emotionally too. You were strong. Many nurses and doctors called you a fighter. Your twisting and flipping inside me only solidified my faith in you and your presence as a living, breathing human. You and I fought hard to get to this point, to finally meet each other and proclaim that we did it. I couldn't imagine a greater satisfaction.

■ ■ ■

Tiny candles lit up the bathroom with dancing flames casting a subtle orange glow. A blue light illuminated the water and invited me in. Scott began to play melodic music on his phone, and the rhythm of the songs combined with the soothing bubbles in the tub sent me into a trance-like state. After a few hours, I felt my contractions strengthen, followed by a warm rush of fluid escaping my body. This was my cue: you were coming.

Almost instantly my stomach started to move. You began turning from posterior to face down in preparation for birth, and we could physically watch as your body twisted into position. All my babies had done this as soon as my water broke but I had never actually felt it before. It was amazing and I marveled at the movement until another contraction blew the breath from my body. Kristin and Scott got me out of the tub and onto the bed but I couldn't find a comfortable position.

In the middle of all this, the telemetry monitors failed and the nurses wanted to put me back on the wired ones. I refused to stay in the bed, so I got on the floor next to the machine and labored there with the peanut ball.

My nurse was flustered with my insistence on being out of bed, and made herself scarce. She was young and obviously inexperienced. Her lack of concern made me wonder what she had heard about our situation. Did she think, like many others, that having you was not my choice or was she simply an introvert, afraid to interact?

The young nurse arrived and asked if I felt like I had to push. I said no so she promptly left the room. At that moment it was the truth, but very shortly afterwards, things suddenly changed.

What happened in the minutes later are a blur. I felt a slight push, an uncontrollable force within my body, and then everything became chaotic.

Kristin paged the nurse, who seemed very relaxed and in no rush to call the doctor. I had another contraction, my body tightened and I screamed. Kristin paged the nurse again, yelling, "The baby is coming now, someone needs to be in here!" and suddenly the volume of noise around me increased dramatically.

The door to our room was only slightly open as I labored on the floor right in front of it, but still a flood of medical staff began rushing in, asking what had happened and why wasn't I moved to an operating room. My young nurse hadn't told anyone I was ready to deliver. I had stopped pushing, afraid of what might occur, when suddenly a face appeared next to me—a female doctor, gloves barely on her hand as she told me to push. I quickly re-focused and bore down.

As your head emerged, you let out a loud, lusty cry. I collapsed on the floor while the rest of your body came in one last contraction.

"She's crying," I sobbed as you were taken across the room to the warmer. "She can breathe."

A wave of relief washed over me and I lay in a heap on the floor.

You had arrived.

> Life is what happens when you are busy making other plans.
>
> —John Lennon

CHAPTER TWO
October 5, 2011

The IVF clinic building was located inside an industrial park off a main highway leading out of Philadelphia. The expansive layout of the stone structure was impressive, covering what looked like a football field in size. The glass windows that lined the front gave a brief look into the inner workings even before you got to the front door. Doctors sat in their offices studying mounds of paperwork, now and then looking out thoughtfully at their surroundings.

Scott pulled into the parking lot and we walked inside, taking the first floor elevator up to my doctor's office.

Seeing the familiar face of the receptionist I checked in, and through the open door I spotted the doctor sitting at his desk. He looked up at me and smiled, easing my nerves.

I shifted uncomfortably in my seat. Why, I wondered, do they insist you come to a clinic appointment with a full bladder? We had been sitting in the waiting room for twenty minutes and I felt like a balloon about to burst.

Eventually my attention fell on Scott, who sat to my left, reading a magazine. There were very few times in our relationship when I had seen him reading; I wondered why he chose this day to drift off into the spurious world of a popular women's magazine when my mind couldn't concentrate on anything other than the momentous procedure I was about to have. As I watched his eyes move across the words, my thoughts began to drift back to the day we first met.

FIVE YEARS EARLIER

At the time we were introduced I had no need for anyone in my life. The desire to find a companion, someone I could fall deeply in love with, just wasn't there anymore. My heart had been broken too many times to let another man in, who in the end would only stomp on my dreams. For a long time all I wanted was someone to love me, but as time passed I had come to the conclusion that I didn't need a partner. I pushed my desire to be a mother to the side and settled for the role of an aunt, which was just fine with me.

"Auntie Crystal," my oldest nephew yelled from inside the tiny living room, "I'm hungry."

I snapped to attention. My nephews were only two and five-years-old and they were always asking for something. Luckily this time I knew exactly what they wanted. I had already started some macaroni and cheese on the stovetop but went over to the pantry to find something to satisfy them for a few minutes longer while the pasta finished cooking. They were watching a movie and always liked to have something to munch on during movie time.

The pantry offered zero options for any sort of easy snack. Discouraged, I went back to the refrigerator and grabbed the last of the grapes. I washed them and put them in a bowl. Both boys grinned as I walked back into the living room, setting the bowl in front of them.

My sister's youngest daughter, a five-month-old ball of smiles, stared at me from her bouncer and made cooing noises. Her tiny hands slammed big, colorful buttons in the shape of baby animals. As she hit each one, bright lights would blink and illuminate the faces of cute little giraffes, lions, and bears. I smiled wistfully; If only life could be so simple again.

■ ■ ■

I walked over to the kitchen table where my laptop sat and decided to look for a new car. In a few days I wouldn't be responsible for my sister's three kids any longer, so the Toyota Camry I had my eyes on was a definite possibility. It was smaller than my Jeep and would get much better gas mileage. I always loved Toyotas, and the Jeep I currently drove had begun to dance across the highway every time we hit a pothole or a bump. I'd had a For Sale sign in the window for a few weeks with no interest yet, but with three children in the car I no longer felt safe driving it.

I scrolled the pages of my local Craigslist site and saw that the Camry was still available. I couldn't afford to buy a new one but the 1991 model I had found would suit me perfectly; it was a standard, equipped with a sunroof, which was much better than the air-conditioning that had stopped working in the Jeep months ago.

As I read through the rest of the description, I picked up my cell phone and dialed Dan's number. He was a mechanic and a good friend of mine. I hoped he could help me figure out if the car was worth the $750 they were asking for it. I certainly didn't need to go buying another clunker. Our conversation was quick and Dan agreed to come and look at it with me. I felt some relief knowing he would be there to give me his honest opinion about my potential purchase.

I heard commotion in the other room as I dumped the cheesy powder for the mac n' cheese into the pot. The boys were wrestling, which meant the movie was over.

"When is lunch going to be ready," my nephew yelled again.

"Hold your horses," I called back. "It'll be ready when it's ready."

I loved having the kids over. Their presence made for a good excuse to get out of the house and do something fun. It had only been a little over four months since my sister went back to work and I enjoyed watching her kids. I wished she had the ability to pay me for my services but I figured that the state assistance she qualified for would eventually kick in and I would be compensated. It was financially stressful having an apartment all on my own with only my nanny job, but I made it work and enjoyed having company in my cozy little place.

A few minutes later the mac n' cheese was ready and I called the boys into the kitchen for lunch so I could go into the other room and call the person who listed the Toyota Camry for sale. My apartment was only quiet when they were eating or at home with my sister.

I dialed the number. "Hello," I said. "My name is Crystal and

I'm calling about the car you advertised on Craigslist."

"Yes. It's for sale. Want it?" the rough voice on the other end asked. He sounded like someone who smoked five packs of cigarettes a day.

"Um, I am interested. Would I be able to come over and take a look at it? I don't live too far from you. Maybe ten minutes."

"Yeah. How 'bout you come today?"

"Sure. What time?"

"How 'bout now?"

"Well I'll have to call my mechanic. He'll be coming with me. How about one o'clock?"

"Okay then, see you at one."

I hung up the phone and called Dan again to tell him what time I needed him. Dan said he would be at my apartment soon, so I quickly got myself together, fixing my hair and slipping on my sandals.

Both children had devoured their lunch, slurping up the last of the cheese sauce with bowls to their faces.

"Put your shoes on," I told the kids as I collected the empty bowls and placed them in the sink. "We're going to get Mommy."

On our way out the door I got another phone call from someone interested in my Jeep. I explained the suspension problem to the guy on the other end of the line, but he said he still wanted to see it. I really needed the money from the Jeep if I was going to be able to buy the Camry, so the phone call couldn't have come at a better time.

We agreed to meet at five p.m., after I had the chance to see the Camry. It was almost one o'clock, and my sister worked a half-hour away. I would have to hurry to make my plan successful. I drove quickly through the back roads, down to the pet store where my sister worked. I needed to drop the kids off with her and get back home in ten minutes to meet Dan.

Dan pulled up to my apartment seconds after I arrived. I vaguely noticed another person in the passenger seat, but didn't pay too much attention. When I got into his car Dan introduced us and I took note of his name, but quickly forgot it as thoughts of selling my Jeep and buying the Camry ran through my mind.

As we drove I was consumed with my thoughts while Dan and the stranger chatted. After a few interjections: "take a right here" and "it's number fifty-two," we finally arrived at the house and they both got out of the car. As I walked around to the front of the car I saw the stranger clearly for the first time. He stood at an average height, maybe 5' 11", with shaved brown hair and a logoed t-shirt, the same shirt I had seen Dan wear from the shop he worked in as a mechanic.

"Hi," he said, hiding his hands in his jeans pockets.

"Hey," I replied, ringing the doorbell. *Damn*, I thought to myself. *I wish I could remember his name.*

"I figured you could use two mechanics to look at this car," Dan said. "And Scott's been a mechanic longer than me."

"The more, the merrier," I replied, thankful that he said his name again.

An older, scruffy looking man answered the door. He led us to a garage, the old style that had to be manually opened and closed. Its faded white paint had chipped off and landed in chunks on the ground at our feet. Inside, an oldish Camry sat, a thin layer of dust covering the hood. Its black exterior was lined with red pin-striping running across the doors. I balked at the colors, but that was the least of my concerns. The outside was in decent condition, just a bit dull and weathered, and I heard the old man tell Dan that he had bought another car a few months earlier and it had been in the garage ever since.

"So, whatcha think?" the man asked, standing with his hands on his hips and a cigarette hanging out of his mouth. He looked as though he hadn't shaved in days and his white v-neck t-shirt had yellow stains underneath his arms and around the collar.

"It's nice," I replied as I looked through the windows at the worn interior. After meeting the owner I had expected the car to be loaded with trash and half-smoked cigarette butts. I was surprised to see that while far from pristine, it was fairly clean.

"Ya want it?"

This man certainly got to the point. "I do. But can I test drive it first?"

"Blown clutch," the man replied. "Can't drive it anywhere. You'll have to get it towed."

"Seems to be in fairly good condition," Dan said, trailing his fingers along the hood of the car.

"It should be. I hardly drive it anywhere," replied the sweaty man. "I'm only selling it 'cuz I can't drive two cars."

"I'll take it," I said, with a smile on my face, handing the man the money I'd saved. Hopefully I'd make it back with the sale of my Jeep that evening.

"Why don't I come with you to get it tomorrow?" Scott asked.

"That would be great," I replied, slightly shocked that this guy I had just met wanted to help me out.

■ ■ ■

As I pulled up to my driveway I noticed someone was already there. I introduced myself as I exited the Jeep, assuming he was the potential buyer. Without even a hello, he handed me the cash from the back left pocket of his jeans. Watching him pull away in the Jeep I'd had for the last year, my mind raced with the happy prospect of driving my new vehicle—one that would actually drive straight and could keep me cool in the hot summer months.

■ ■ ■

After making a couple of phone calls, I threw on my sneakers and walked the block and a half around the corner to my sister's apartment. The night was so beautiful I didn't even miss having a car. Walking the short distance, I thought about the new advantages of having a vehicle that didn't break down all the time. My pace quickened and I found myself almost skipping. Nearing her apartment, I could see her watching for me through her basement-level apartment door, a smile lighting her face as I got closer.

"So, did you buy it?" she asked, opening the door.

"Yup," I said, squeezing through the barely open entrance so that her dog didn't escape.

Lisette, my sister by choice, stood and gave me a hug. Usually I was the one to initiate the embrace, so it was nice to see this type of unprompted affection.

She was my best friend and soul sister, younger than me by a little over two years. Her life had never been easy: abandoned by her mother at thirteen, a mother herself at seventeen, and trapped in an abusive relationship for more years than I care to recall. Although we were separated for about fifteen years when as a child my family was uprooted, we reconnected when her second baby was only a few months old and quickly rekindled our friendship, establishing an unshakable bond. Rarely did more than a few days pass between phone calls or visits, and I had bailed her out of numerous bad situations in the past. Our relationship had always been strange; mutually beneficial but unequal at the same time. When times got tough I had consistently been the protector, the one to seek out solutions, or had come to the rescue when she desperately needed saving. We both dreamed of the day when we would have the money and resources to give our children better than we currently had.

But Lisette suffered from depression and anxiety. Her demons were much more influential than my own childhood depressive episodes had ever been. As much as I wanted to help her, to save her from the darkness she saw everywhere, I needed her to save me from my own evils. Her nurturing, and the love and care of her children, kept me from becoming encumbered with the thoughts that I would never have my own children. We were each other's motivation and inspiration.

As I left her house later that night, I tried to envision what the perfect scenario would be for the five of us—my sister, her three kids and me. I truly thought that at some point we would all be creating a life for ourselves together, without the need for a man to support us. I've always been very independent and it seemed simpler to create the life we wanted without the complication of another person's feelings or opinions. Coming from a blended family and having witnessed my own mother's struggles with married life, I had never been big on the idea of marriage. But I did miss the companionship of having someone around to talk to, and thought that the concept of a loving and supportive family was important, especially for the benefit of my own children. I still wasn't sure about how I felt when it came to opening up my heart again, but I decided that maybe I was ready for a little companionship.

■ ■ ■

The next day I called Scott and asked him to come over early. The kids were all at my house again, and I felt that if I didn't have some adult interaction, I might start to go a bit insane. They were playing with Matchbox cars when my doorbell rang.

"Hi," he said, standing on my front porch.

"Thanks for coming over earlier. I'm so bored and thought you might want to hang out for a bit before we went over to get the car."

"Well, I don't have anything better to do."

Scott made his way to the couch and sat next to my oldest nephew.

"Wanna watch a movie with us?" he asked.

"Sure," Scott said.

"You make yourself comfortable. I'm going to get us some sodas," I said, exiting the living room towards the kitchen.

When I came back, Scott had placed my five-month-old niece on his chest. Never one to accept a stranger's arms willingly, she was nestled with her head on his shoulder, fast asleep. I tried not to make it obvious, but suddenly this stranger had entered my life and burrowed his way into my heart, a heart I had barricaded from any sort of outside interest. This little baby, who didn't know Scott at all, trusted him enough to fall quickly asleep on his broad chest without any hesitation whatsoever. He looked up at me and smiled, a small smile, enough to suggest he had caught me staring. I turned away, but soon looked back to watch him gazing at my sleeping niece with such peace and warmth in his eyes that my heart melted.

As I stood in the doorway, watching them on the couch, I caught a vision of my future. I truly hoped it was a future dowsed in reality and not another fantasy of mine.

SAVING STORMIE: THE BABY S STORY

"Crystal," a nurse called from an open door to the right of where Scott and I sat, catapulting me back to the present. It had been good to think of something other than my bursting bladder.

Scott grabbed my hand as I stood up from my chair. "It'll work," he said.

I looked down at him and smiled, taking a deep breath as I headed towards the nurse, hoping with every part of my soul that Scott was right.

Pregnant...

I mouthed the special word silently to myself.

If it works I will be pregnant...

> Dispassionate
> objectivity is
> itself a passion,
> for the real
> and for the truth.
>
> —Abraham Maslow

CHAPTER THREE
August, 2000

I chose to defy my mother one too many times and this time meant I'd be living on the street, but maybe that was the best thing that could happen to me.

At nineteen I'm not a baby anymore, I told myself as I carried my bags out to the car. I'd be on my own, absent of her control. In many ways my mother's stubborn nature sent me into a frenzied rage, but I also saw the same traits looming in myself and that scared me even more. I never wanted to have this type of capricious relationship with anyone, but as time went on it seemed inevitable, and being kicked out vindicated those feelings.

Although my mother and I had a rocky relationship, I always felt as though I could talk to her about anything. But this time I really screwed up. It happened when I was nineteen and dropped out of college. She did not like me leaving school and coming back to live with her in St. Louis, but after the year I'd had we both agreed it was the best decision. In college I experienced my first taste of freedom so I was not willing to accept the same restrictions I had before I left home. I was what she considered to be rebellious, battling my own demons internally and exposing those demons by defying her hopes and wishes.

Dealing with the sadness the last few months had brought, and wrestling with the desire to simply forget my entire college experience, left me emotionless and void of ambition to make anything better. It was all I could manage to get out of bed each day. She kept telling me I needed to find a job. Like most mothers, she wanted to fix me. But her protective glue could only hold me together for so long. My inner struggles were pushing back her expectations with relentless force, and did not create a cohesive environment for two people living together. By the end of most days, I just wanted to run away. There were many nights when I was able to escape, but each time I returned I could see the look on her face. I recognize it now as disappointment, but at the time she seemed to regard me with critical judgment and I wanted no part of it.

One night when I told her I had planned to go out with some of my friends, she said I had to be back at seven. It was absurd. What nineteen-year-old had to be home by seven at night? I blew off her curfew with little thought. We were having fun, cruising around in my friend's vintage muscle car with the radio blasting and the windows down. When I was with them it didn't matter where we were or who we were with; nobody there wanted to talk about my goals for the future or how much I was screwing up by dropping out of college and not getting a job.

I fell asleep at one point, curled up in the back of the Chevelle. By two a.m. I knew I wasn't going home, so I crashed with one of my friends and waited for morning. Daylight emerged and brought with it the realization that I was going to have to face reality for another day. While everyone slept I crept quietly around the house, enjoying the peace and serenity while fighting off the anxiety that started to rise in my chest. I dreaded the guilt my mother would load on me. I could hear her now: *What if you were lying in a ditch somewhere? How would I know?*

Is a ditch so bad? I asked myself. Surely there were things much worse than being stuck in a hole somewhere. It would certainly be better than what I was about to endure when I eventually walked through the front door.

I returned home at noon, and gathering every bit of determination I could find, hoping she wasn't standing in the living room waiting for me, I turned the key in the lock. As soon as the tumblers clicked, all the little noises that had been coming from inside the house stopped. *Shit*, I thought, *there goes my chance of sneaking in quietly and reaching my room before she noticed.*

I walked in slowly, very aware of the eyes that were focused on me. Expecting an explosion at any moment, I braced myself and looked up. Her stony face gave away nothing, but her eyes seemed to be sad—something I did not understand.

She didn't say anything when she saw me enter through the front door. But in a cluster by the living room coffee table, she had all my things packed up in bags. I stared at her and she stared back, holding a piece of paper in her right hand by her side.

"Hi, Mom," I said. "What's going on?"

"You need to leave this house."

She looked at me, her face stoic and unreadable, unlike the many other times we got into a fight.

"I'm serious, Crystal," she said with her hands on her hips and her lips pursed together, a clear sign to me that she was beyond mad. "This is it. I can't save you anymore. I gave you a roof over your head and you give me a three hundred dollar phone bill."

"You're kicking me out? Over a phone bill!"

"It's for your own good."

It seemed ironic to me that my mother, a well-respected and intelligent nurse in the St. Louis area, who cared for all her patients with the deepest sympathy and compassion, stood before me, telling me to get out of her house.

"For my own good?" I shouted at her. "Where am I supposed to go?"

"That's not my problem anymore. You consistently defy me, and this time you need to see what it takes to survive on your own. I won't be your crutch any longer."

I stood there for what seemed like hours, but only seconds had passed. My thoughts were racing but no words would come out. Defeated, I picked up the three bags at my feet and walked out, slamming the door behind me.

My friend who had dropped me off was still parked in front of the house. He helped me put my bags into the trunk and asked me what I was going to do. I told him to take me back to where we had slept the night before. I would figure it all out tomorrow, but for now I needed to escape. Again.

EIGHT YEARS LATER

This lonely feeling was one I would experience many times as the years went by. It seemed as though, no matter how hard I tried, I was often faced with the reality that I was on my own.

As I sat on my sister's couch waiting for Scott to emerge from the bathroom, I thought about how our lives would change if my instincts were correct. The lingering nausea I had begun to feel and the tenderness in my breasts could not be just because it was around that time of the month. I felt different, emotionally and physically. I'd had this feeling before. And like every other time, I faced it alone. I knew if I had to I would do it by myself once again, but the prospect still scared me. My eyes had just begun to fill with tears when the door opened.

As Scott came out of the bathroom, my sister grabbed my hand. His face turned a pale shade of white and he nodded, tilting his head down, then looking back up at me. Our eyes met and I knew he had confirmed my beliefs. Nine months from now we would be parents, hopefully, but I wondered if he would stick around to meet the baby boy or girl. Through years of believing I would never be a mother I had always daydreamed about finding out I was pregnant again. I often wondered if a man would be in the picture. To me that wasn't an important aspect of the pregnancy. However, I had decided long ago that if a pregnancy were to occur unexpectedly, I would at least give the other person the option of being in the child's life or walking away. My decision to have a child was not dependent on the involvement of the child's father, but I didn't know how Scott felt about that.

We sat in silence for a long time before he asked me what I was thinking. Out of nowhere I blurted out, "Please don't ask me to get rid of it. I won't!" He looked startled, and nodded.

"I wouldn't ask you to," he said, kissing me on the forehead. "We can try to make this work. Even if we can't make it as a couple, we'll do it as friends."

Just like the day my mother kicked me out, I felt completely
alone despite the presence of Scott beside me. We hadn't even been
dating for a full month yet. The deepest conversation we'd had up
to this point was about what movie we were going to watch. How
were we supposed to raise a child together? He smiled at me, but
his smile only lasted a few seconds, then he turned away and stared
at the wall. We sat in silence for a few moments until my sister
announced that dinner was ready. As we went into the kitchen to
get our food, I caught Scott staring at me. When he saw me looking
back, his eyes quickly averted. I wondered what was going through
his head.

While I was happy to have Scott by my side through the
pregnancy, I wasn't thrilled that we were together just to 'make this
work.' I wanted more than someone bound to me by a child. We
hadn't had the time yet to fall in love or talk about what we wanted
for our future together. Now we had no choice. Everything seemed
so forced.

■　■　■

After my mother kicked me out at nineteen, I lived a life
I would never wish on anyone. To keep a roof over my head I
worked for impoverished families as a live-in nanny. One of those
families nearly cost me my life due to their involvement with
drugs. I met many people whose intentions seemed good, but
in reality they were out to exploit me; to build me up just to let
me down. It was at those moments that I became stronger than I
thought I could ever be.

My mother's choice to send me into the streets of St. Louis
nearly broke me and I faced some of the darkest times I can

remember, but it also created a very important part of who I became. I learned to survive on my own; I learned that nobody but I myself could truly keep me from accomplishing what I wanted in life. At the same time I also developed skin so thick that no one could pierce it. I built a protective armor around myself, impenetrable to any outside force. My experiences taught me that the ones who got close to me had the ability to hurt me the most, so I had to protect myself from every type of attachment, especially the love of a man.

Now, standing in the next room, was someone I wasn't even sure I wanted to take a chance on. But for the sake of the child I had wished for, the child I had wanted for so many years, he was. I only hoped he would also be the one to tear down my walls and make me believe in love again.

Choices
are the hinges
of destiny.

—Pythagoras

CHAPTER FOUR
March, 2011

grabbed the freshly printed pages out of the tray of my printer. Six crisp white forms with question after question stared back at me. They invited me to tell the story of my life.

I walked across the cool tile floor to my kitchen table. As I pulled out the chair I wondered how long it would take to write down my answers. I needed to be thorough but I was also anxious about how my words would be received. So many weeks and months of waiting were finally coming to an end. The anticipation in the pit of my stomach grew as I scanned the questions asked. They were intrusive, invading every deeply personal event I had ever experienced.

The bright sunlight streaming in my kitchen window

reflected off my glasses as I took them off and placed them on the table. I needed a moment to gather myself before I started on the documents before me. As I grabbed them from the smooth surface of the table and went to look for a pen, a thought crossed my mind. Finally, I thought, this might actually happen.

■　■　■

The decision came easily. I had heard about surrogacy when I was much younger, mainly from celebrities using surrogates, but did not know anyone personally who had either been a surrogate or had searched for one. As soon as I began to look into the process, I knew I wanted to pursue it. I also knew I wanted to be pregnant again but that Scott and I should not embark on parenthood any further than our first two daughters. The introduction of Emmy into our lives had been a significant challenge and I felt as though the exhaustion in caring for two children had already reached its limit. Yet I still wanted to provide the happiness I had received from having Anne and Emmy to another woman or couple who could not have children of their own.

Pregnancy was easy for me and I loved the way it made me feel, especially in the second trimester when my energy returned and I could anticipate meeting my baby for the first time. Being able to experience pregnancy without the responsibility of caring for a newborn, however, seemed very appealing. And because I would have a positive impact on the lives of another family, carrying a baby for other people seemed like the perfect compromise.

A few months after I had Emmy I started missing my pregnant body: the glow to my skin and the feeling of a baby

moving inside me. We lived more naturalistic lives at that time, so I
was no longer on birth control and feared that within a few months
I would be pregnant again, leaving me with another child to care
for in addition to the two I already had. I didn't trust any natural
methods of birth control and wasn't willing to go back on hormonal
medication, so I began to pursue other alternatives.

It wasn't difficult, Stormie. I sat down at my laptop and
started my search with Google. It led me to the sites of a few local
agencies and to a members-only forum called Surrogatemother.
com. I clicked on the link and was instantly given the option to
create a profile and post in the welcome boards, letting people
know who I was and why I was visiting. There were different
boards for multiple categories of people: Intended parents,
surrogates, international surrogacy, traditional surrogacy, and
gestational surrogacy. Through my research I realized I wanted
to participate in gestational surrogacy and did not want any
biological ties to any child I carried. I felt that the binds of biology
might influence my emotional state later on. Pages and pages of
information displayed before me but I sat for a few hours reading
through all the posts. Most were positive and reassured me that
this was the path I wanted to journey down.

■   ■   ■

I checked the boards daily, often reading the 'Surrogate
Wanted' ads for people who were nearby. I began to notice that
a lot of agents posted on the boards on behalf of their clients. I
decided to contact each of the agencies that made more than one
posting, and await a response. Within a day I had talked to four
different agencies, yet due to my possession of Medicaid, only

one determined that I was eligible for the surrogacy program. Frustrated, I wondered if I would ever be able to play a role in the creation of a family.

I started thinking about egg donation and the possibility of serving as an independent surrogate with the intended family paying for my insurance.

Quite a few months passed before anything happened. I had all but given up on my idea of being a surrogate. Every email I got from a surrogacy agent and the new postings that appeared on the boards filled me with the longing to help, but I didn't know how any of it would work out.

I emailed back some of the agencies I had spoken with previously, asking them to reconsider my application. None of them would make any exceptions. They told me to call back when I was independent.

Eventually an email appeared in my inbox, not in my surrogatemother.com account, but in my personal email. One of the agents I had sent an inquiry to was interested in learning more about me and my desire to carry a child for someone. I wrote back, describing my situation, telling her about the struggle I'd had with getting approved from other agencies. I never expected to hear from her again, but a few days later I received a response.

That shouldn't be a problem, the email read. From the signature I could tell the sender was a woman from a small agency based out of Pennsylvania. She gave me her phone number and urged me to call her at my earliest convenience.

I left Scott on the couch and went into the kitchen to call the surrogacy agency. A woman with a lovely voice answered the phone, her words soft and gentle. She introduced herself as Sharon. We talked for a few minutes and she told me about a man who was waiting for a match. He was foreign-born and English-speaking. She explained that he would be pursuing surrogacy alone, without a partner, and that he had a deep desire to start a family.

Sharon told me that I would need to fill out some paperwork in order to make the matches official, but she believed I was a good candidate. She would send me an email attaching the official application packet, along with a list of required tests to be updated before beginning the in vitro fertilization procedure.

■　■　■

"Do you really want to go through with this?" Lisette asked, nervously tapping her feet on the floor of my kitchen.

"You know me," I said. "I wouldn't be at the point of calling an agency if I didn't want to go through with it."

"Okay, but what does Scott think?" she whispered.

"He's... he's a bit apprehensive to say the least."

"What are you going to tell the girls?"

"Nothing yet. I just started this process. There isn't anything to tell."

Lisette's youngest daughter and Emmy were busy playing together on the floor of my living room. They were only four months apart and got along like sisters. Lisette, like Scott, didn't understand why I would want to carry someone else's child and was fearful that I would grow attached to the baby, leaving me apprehensive when the time came to give up the baby to its rightful parents after birth.

Scott and Lisette weren't alone in their concerns. My mother also had apprehensions of her own.

My mom had, in my mind, always been one of the biggest doubters I had in my life. We had never really gotten along when

I lived under her roof. I always felt judged and intimidated. But after having my first child, our relationship changed. Perhaps it was because we lived so far apart, or maybe it was because I was a mother myself, as her attitude towards me changed drastically when Anne entered our lives. Instead of belittling me, she encouraged me, and I often found myself calling her to get her advice on the things that meant the most to me. When I decided to become a doula she became one of my biggest supporters and later helped me with my business plan for a career I hoped would one day become a reality.

I came to rely on her opinions, but this decision I made was one she couldn't quite understand.

"Aren't you scared?" I could hear my mother's voice shake as she spoke to me on the phone. "I can't imagine you're going to feel okay giving away a baby."

"Mom, I've worked with other people's kids for how long? I can love a kid from a distance. I've done it with dozens of children over the last ten years."

"You're right," she admitted.

I knew I was right. Years of experience in childcare had not come without more than a couple of children who truly pulled at my heart. In 1999 I cared for a little boy who was born addicted to drugs. At nine months he could not sit or play on his own and I needed to be right next to him every minute of every day. Then there was the young girl I transported back and forth to daycare every day when her mother had back surgery. Each of those kids had been special to me and had grown up, living their own lives without me by their side.

"To some extent, this baby will be in my life forever. It will be awesome to see what kind of person it grows up to be, unlike the children I've cared for in the past."

"That is one really positive benefit, Crystal. I give you a lot of credit. I know you're a devoted mother, but to think about doing this for someone else... you have a really big heart. I hope you know that I'm proud of you."

Others were not so understanding but I didn't really care about their objections. I believed in my heart that I was destined to be a surrogate. As long as I could get through the pregnancy without developing an attachment, I would be fine. I had done that in the past and didn't see much difference. Just like when a child came into the daycare centers where I once worked, I knew that at some point they would be going home.

■　■　■

"Well, it looks like I'm really going to do this," I said, walking back into the room where Scott had turned on the television, frantically flipping through channels.

"You know I'd support you no matter what, so whatever you need me to do, you let me know," he said, brimming with a delicate smile. I smiled back and turned to walk into the kitchen. I knew he was hesitant but I was excited about the possibilities.

A few days later I received the promised packet, emailed from Sharon. I opened it and immediately printed off the forms. The personality sheet asked questions like, "Would you consider yourself a caring person?" And, "When was your last intimate relationship?" The questions delved into areas of my life few people really knew about.

I grabbed my pen and, despite my apprehension, began to fill out each line, sometimes anxious about revealing the truth, often wondering if my answers would be a detriment to my goal. Sharon had said that the paperwork was mostly a formality, but since my

CHAPTER FOUR

relationship with Scott had been shaky at times, I was still nervous and I did not have a strong financial background to showcase.

I glanced through the list of questions, wondering how it would be best to answer them. I knew some of my answers were not what would typically be considered ideal for surrogacy. However, my conversation with Sharon left me feeling like I had already been accepted.

Question 1: Why do you want to be a surrogate?

Question 3: How many children do you have?

Question 6: Do you have insurance? What kind? Does it cover maternity?

Question 11: Do you have a stable source of income?

Question 17: What is your relationship status? If you are not married and/or in a relationship, describe the stability of that relationship.

I must be clear and straightforward. There are those who believe I pursued surrogacy for the money, and that I was a single mother in need of financial support when I started this process. It was true that I did not have a lot on my own, but I did have a job, and I did have a relationship with Scott. I worked as a nanny for a family in a beautiful northern Connecticut neighborhood and had flexibility and a good source of income. Scott worked full time as a mechanic, so we always had the money for our rent and utilities, with sometimes extra to spend on treats.

I couldn't complain about the financial situation I was in when I began pursuing surrogacy. Our relationship was never perfect, but we stuck together through our challenges and worked hard at providing a good, stable, loving environment for our children to grow up in.

I eventually reached the final question on the page:

Question 24: What do you plan to do with the monies from your surrogacy fee?

Well, at least one question was easy. I'd had a dream for the last five to six years of opening a holistic family center where parents and babies could learn all about each other in a safe and informative environment, offering services such as massage, doulas, chiropractic care, and acupuncture—all things I believed in and had seen work. Finding a place to marry my particular interest areas of doula work and the management of postpartum depression, I had come up with the idea for a family center specializing in women at risk of postpartum depression, using a holistic model of care. I'd had the training for the business formation and management, as well as being certified as a doula. I had just been searching for the means.

Surrogacy was the perfect solution. I would have an extra sum of money to invest into the business. It was all a great plan. In addition, not only would I gain a realization of a business dream, but also the joy of having another child who was a part of my world, even if only through contact with the parents. I did not need nor want another child to take care of but I wouldn't object to another niece or nephew.

I read through all the questions on the application and realized there was one more I had not yet answered. Dread filled the pit of my stomach. This question could make or break everything:

Question 18: How many children do you have? How many pregnancies?

CHAPTER FOUR

> That which does
> not kill us makes
> us stronger.
>
> —Friedrich
> Nietzsche

CHAPTER FIVE
February 12, 2001

Sharp pain pierced through my legs and torso, forcing my body to fold over in agony. I felt a pop and a rush of fluid run down my thighs. I hoped I could muster up the strength to drag myself to my roommate's truck and drive to the closest hospital.

At eighteen, I was alone and unsure of what was happening to me. I had left my hometown in Missouri for a small college town in Kentucky. While there, I discovered I was pregnant. The father was a boyfriend I'd had for several years, but he was never reliable or even consistent. I knew I was on my own and was determined to get through the pregnancy alone, living as a single mother after the baby's birth.

I sobbed as I hobbled down the stairs and out to the vehicle parked much too far away for my failing body. I began to hyperventilate and tried to take in deep breaths to calm myself down. I practically fell into the truck, leaning on it for support, unsure how much longer my legs could hold me. I gripped the handle of the truck and let out a loud shriek, releasing the pent up tension of the past few minutes.

A figure appeared from the edge of my vision and asked if I was okay. I nodded, unable to muster any words. I wasn't sure how I would drive myself almost a half hour away to the hospital, but somehow I had to build up the strength to do so. The shadowy figure told me the campus clinic might be able to help and for a moment I felt relief.

I got into the driver's seat and started the truck. The journey took almost ten minutes when it should have taken two, but I had to stop often to regain control and fight back the intense pain slicing through my abdomen.

I pulled right up to the front entrance and saw a nurse inside shutting off some lights, preparing to close down for the night. I tumbled out of the high cabin of the vehicle, my legs barely holding me up. The noise caught the attention of the nurse, who rushed out to hold me up and walk me into the clinic.

"Thank you," I said, hobbling arm in arm with my kind savior.

She yelled to another nurse inside but I could not comprehend anything they were saying in their efforts to subdue my pain.

Two nurses brought me to the closest room they could find and laid me down on an examining table. My body immediately tightened and I sprang up to a seated position. They pulled off my blood-soaked pants and I felt another gush of fluid escape my body. My stomach tightened again and an uncontrollable push forced something from between my legs. I sat up further and tried to see what had been ejected from me. A tiny baby, covered in blood, lay helplessly in front of me. She was much too small to survive. Her little limbs, no larger than three inches, moved slightly as I stared down at her.

Miranda, I cried inwardly, for that was the name I had decided upon if she was a girl, *Oh my little Miranda...* "Help her!" I yelled. "Please, can you help her?"

"Oh, Honey," one of the nurses said, trying to pick her up and take her away.

But I slapped her hand and gingerly lifted up my baby girl.

She continued to move in little itty-bitty motions and I thought I saw her chest rise and fall but it could have been my hopeful wish for her survival. I sat with her for a few minutes and cried until her arms and legs stopped moving and her body went limp.

Only my absent boyfriend at the time knew I was pregnant. There wasn't anyone else I could turn to. I couldn't tell my parents that I miscarried or that I was even pregnant. I was supposed to be starting a new life for myself by going to college. How could I let them down again?

I don't remember how I got there, but I awoke in my dorm room. For the next two, maybe three, days I slept, never leaving the confines of my bed. My baby's tiny body appeared in every dream, every thought I had. Nothing mattered anymore. I had made many bad decisions in the months prior to the miscarriage, and her loss sent me spiraling into a deep depression. I stopped going to my classes and drank my sorrows away at any party

I could find. Finally, when the semester ended and the warm summer air moved in, I went back to live with my mother who immediately saw the distress I was in. She admitted me to an outpatient program and it was there that I tried to erase the last few months of my tormented life—and the visions of my Miranda's fragile little body.

■　■　■

Years later, when I went to see an obstetrician, I was told that due to the damage the miscarriage had caused, I might never have children of my own. I was devastated at this news, and decided I would care for other people's children. The escape became my sad attempt at living vicariously through couples who were able to have their own. I wanted kids so badly and saw no hope of that ever occurring.

Thankfully, I was eventually able to have children, but that experience altered me forever: I was able to understand the sorrow a miscarriage could bring a woman, who by every natural right should be able to have a child if she chose to do so. It was what led intrinsically to my passionate desire not to let another hopeful mother feel the pain I had felt.

MARCH, 2011

My hands shook as I wrote down my answer to question eighteen. Tears streamed down my face as I thought about my baby's tiny body moving in my arms, taking her last breath as I gazed at her little face, longing for her eyes to open. But my wishes had gone unheard. I didn't want to be too detailed about my experience, but I also wasn't going to lie. Describing the miscarriage, I chose my words carefully, fully aware that my honesty could be my downfall.

I sent my completed application to Sharon and waited. Days passed before I finally received a phone call.

I had been approved.

> When one
> door closes,
> another opens.
>
> —Alexander
> Graham Bell

CHAPTER SIX
April, 2011

"**N**ow that you're officially approved, I'd like to talk to you about a possible match," Sharon said when she phoned me. "His name is Mark and he wants to embark in surrogacy on his own. He's desperate to start a family."

For two days Mark and I tried to connect, playing phone tag before he finally reached me while Scott and I were wandering aimlessly around Babies R' Us looking for a dress for Emmy's first birthday party.

"Hello, Crystal?" Mark said. His voice resonated with a foreign accent; he sounded French but it was hard to tell where he was from since he had obviously been educated in the English language.

"Hi, Mark. How are you?" I said, as Scott and I meandered in and out of the racks of clothing, passing by anything over twenty dollars.

"Just fine," he replied.

Scott held up a beautiful purple, short sleeve outfit that had an attached tulle skirt.

She'd love it, I thought to myself and gave Scott the thumbs up.

We walked to the front of the store where the registers were. Lines of people filled the open checkout lanes as I tried to concentrate on the conversation with Mark. Scott waited in line as I held the phone away from my mouth, covering the bottom part of it so Mark wouldn't hear me telling Scott I was going to sit in the car.

We talked for over an hour. He told me about his hopes for a family, and as he spoke, my hesitation about carrying a child for a single man rather than a family quickly slipped away. Mark had been so busy helping to build a successful business that he had not had the time to settle down and find the perfect someone. I had the slight feeling that he was, perhaps, gay, but it didn't really matter. He wanted a child as much as any woman did. I could hear from the excitement in his voice, and the way he described his perfect family, that he would make a great parent. He spoke of his loved ones back in his home country and said that if we were to be successful he would fly me over there every couple of years so I could see the child we created. By the end of the phone call I knew I had made the right choice.

After we hung up I called Sharon. "He sounds like an amazing guy. I'd love to move forward."

She made all the necessary arrangements and a few days later Scott and I met Mark at a Panera Bread in a nearby town.

We walked through the doors of the restaurant and towards

the back we saw a man in an orange golf shirt. When he saw Scott and me, he stood and waved us towards him.

From the moment we sat down we clicked. He wanted to adopt after the surrogacy, or possibly use the same surrogate to have another child. Scott and Mark talked playfully about who would be my 'baby daddy.' The lighthearted conversation put aside every doubt I had.

Three days later Sharon sent me a contract to read over. I asked her if I should have a lawyer look at it.

"That's not necessary," she said. "It's been drafted by a lawyer. If you have any objections, then please let me know and we will change it."

As I looked through page after page I made some notes about questions and alterations I wanted to see in the final draft before I signed it. I called Mark and asked what his thoughts were about termination. His response was that unless it was going to be detrimental to my health to carry the child to term, he did not want any selective reductions. He also told me he was leaning towards a three embryo transfer to increase the likelihood of success the first time around. I was happy he was so excited and told him that, while I was nervous about carrying triplets, if that happened I would be able and willing to do so. We built in a payment schedule for a triplet pregnancy and some stipulations for extras if I did become pregnant with three babies, such as additional childcare and housecleaning to make things easier for me. He wanted to make sure I was as comfortable as possible throughout the entire process.

Mark hoped the embryo transfer could be performed in the summer. He didn't want to get too close to the holidays since he planned to travel back to his hometown during that time. Sharon suggested I use my current insurance to get most of the preliminary medical workups done. It had been over a year since my last OB/ GYN examination, and that needed to be up-to-date along with STD testing before we could start working with the fertility clinic to begin the transfer.

My insurance covered all the tests since they were routine. A few, however, needed to be repeated, so Mark paid those out of his own pocket directly to my doctor's practice. Since Medicaid was not intended for the care I would need going forward, Mark agreed to purchase other insurance for me as well.

Before we could get much further into the insurance issue, the testing was completed and the clinic was contacted, moving the process along. I began daily injections that were required for four weeks prior to embryo transfer. This was an especially exciting time, except that the medications made me very easily agitated. I kept telling myself every day that it would be over soon and I would be pregnant. It would all be worth it if I could give Mark a child. That thought kept me going through all my hormonal changes and the daily injections I had to perform myself.

I remember going over to my neighbor's house across the street more than once, desperate for a break from the confines of my own home. She listened compassionately and always reminded me that my emotional ups and downs were a reaction to the artificial hormones, which my body had not been exposed to in over ten years. I longed for the day I would be off the medications, when my body could adjust to the pregnancy without all the foreign elements.

Two weeks after I started the hormone cycle regime, I went into a local clinic for a baseline ultrasound. I didn't understand why they wanted to do it after I had already started the medication, and since I didn't know much about the process I felt I couldn't question their tactics. When I went home after the ultrasound, Sharon had left an anxious voicemail on my phone, followed by another from the clinic, neither of which were very clear, so I called Sharon for clarification.

"They think they have found something wrong with your uterus. Have you ever had trouble getting pregnant?"

"Both my kids were unplanned," I responded "So no, not really."

"Well, they think you may have fibroids. It's not that big a deal. If you had them you most likely would have had trouble getting pregnant in the past. It will just require a test at your doctor's clinic and then we can get back to the cycle."

"What do you mean? That we won't be going forward?"

"Well there's no point in going forward if you have fibroids. If you do, then the doctors will be able to schedule a procedure to get rid of them, and then you can be approved for IVF cycle. If you don't have them, then there will be no hold-up."

I was stunned. We were already two weeks into the cycle medications. We already had a prospective transfer date set. Now they were saying I had to get a test done before they could move forward and they wanted me to stop taking the medication. Even worse, Mark was not going to pay for the test they needed me to have in order to move forward. I felt like things were starting to fall apart.

When I called the doctor's practice, they told me it would take a minimum of three weeks to schedule an appointment for the test that would determine if I had fibroids or not. A sonohysterogram was something only done in the main clinic and there was very limited availability. I took the earliest possible appointment and emailed Sharon, Mark, and the clinic representative I had been dealing with. Both Sharon and the clinic representative emailed me back right away.

■ ■ ■

The procedure went smoothly and the doctors determined that whatever they had seen in the initial ultrasound that made them believe I had fibroids was erroneous, but it did not matter at that point. The clinic and the agency were at odds about my eligibility to continue in the program. When I tried to sort out who was having the problem, I received many mixed messages from both of them. In the meantime, my emails and phone calls to Mark went unanswered. I felt the same type of let-down I had experienced when trying to find an agency a few short months ago. This time, though, it was exacerbated by the fact that we were quickly approaching what I had anticipated as being our transfer date and I saw my chances of surrogacy slipping away.

I never heard from Mark again.

> But what do
> we know of
> the heart nearest
> to our own?
> What do we
> know of our
> own heart?
>
> —Amelia Barr

CHAPTER SEVEN
July, 2011

I t was a week since I emailed Mark with the news that my sonohysterogram came back without any indication of fibroids. I thought he would at least reply to tell me he had changed his mind.

I found myself crying at the smallest things and often doing a whole lot of nothing, finding little interest in anything I would normally be excited about. I could not comprehend why nothing was working out as I had planned. Mark and I seemed to have a great connection, yet the recent events left me feeling defeated. I could not concentrate on anything but the current situation, and I felt my chance of becoming a surrogate slipping away. I had been so close, and on the day of my anticipated embryo transfer I sat on my couch and stared out the window, dreaming of what I could have been doing instead of feeling sorry for myself. I always liked having a plan so the current circumstances left me feeling completely out of control.

By the middle of July I'd had enough. I needed to move forward, hopefully in the direction to help someone else. I called Sharon to see if there was anything we could do, or if she had any alternative suggestions.

"I'm glad you called this morning. I was going to call you today anyway because I might have another couple for you to help. If you still want to do this."

"I do. Of course I do."

"I mean, it really is your choice. We can wait for Mark to call back, but if he hasn't already I'm not sure he's going to. I have other couples we can look at."

"Well, if you don't hold much hope that he's going to respond, then I don't see the point in waiting."

"Good. I'm not in the office right at this moment but I'll send you all the details about them later this evening. Sound good?"

"Yup. Thanks."

The conversation was short, but it was all I needed. I was ready to move on and find someone else to carry for. The thought of starting my search over terrified me, but I still had hope that it would all work out.

JULY 25, 2011

SUBJECT: Another Couple

Hi Crystal,

Here is the information I promised you on the other couple I told you about earlier. They are a married couple from New York who have three children already. They really want to have another child and have two frozen embryos left over from previous inseminations. They'd like to secure a surrogate quickly because they will need to either pay to store these embryos or discard them. Since you already have your tests completed, we can move this along as fast as possible. Please let me know if it would be okay to pass on your phone number to them so they can contact you.

Thanks,
Sharon

I wrote back a quick email letting Sharon know that would be fine and sat quietly in my bedroom for a few minutes. I was nervous about starting all over again. The other match had seemed so perfect. I still very much wanted to be a surrogate but I wished secretly that Mark would call back to say he was ready to try again.

I lay on my bed, running my hands through my thin brown hair as I stared up at the ceiling. I prepared my list of questions in my head for the new intended parents and readied myself to decide, yet again, whether this potential match would be a good one.

■　■　■

Hours later I heard my phone ringing from inside the kitchen. I turned off the television in the living room and ran to answer it.

"Hi, Crystal. We have you on speaker. I hope that's okay?" the soft female voice said on the other end.

CHAPTER SEVEN

"Yes, that's fine," I replied.

"My name is Ursula and my husband Roger is here with me. Sharon asked us to contact you because we'd like to find a surrogate pretty quickly and we understand you have been cleared with all the tests required."

"Yes, I had a cycle cancelled a few weeks ago, so I'm all set to go."

"We'd like to meet you if that's possible," Ursula said.

"I'd like that, too. When is a good time?"

"Would this weekend be too soon? We have three children and Sharon said you have children around the same age. Maybe we could come to you and meet at a park somewhere so the children can play together and we can have the chance to talk for a while and get to know one another," Ursula suggested.

"This weekend would be great. Where are you coming from? How long would it take to get here."

"Sharon gave us your general location," Roger said. "You live near Manchester, Connecticut, right? We've already mapped it out and it should take just over five hours."

"That's a long drive for you with small children."

"Oh, we don't mind. We desperately want another child and you're kind of our last hope," Ursula said, her voice shaking as she spoke.

"If you're sure it's not too far. There's a beautiful park a few minutes from my house. Maybe we could meet right at the entrance tomorrow. Say two o'clock. That should give you enough time to get here."

"That's perfect. We'll see you at two, then," Roger said.

I rattled off the address of the park and started thinking about the meeting. The location was close enough for me to walk there comfortably, and it was right after Emmy's usual nap, so the girls would be eager to get outside anyway.

■ ■ ■

Roger lifted Emmy into the baby swing and gave her a few gentle pushes, sending her higher and higher into the sky. Her high-pitched laugh made me smile as I watched Roger interact with her. I felt a twinge of resentment, wishing Scott was more involved in family events like this. Lately he was always working and we had seen very little of him.

Ursula took a swig of water from a plastic bottle. "Roger is a very good father."

"I can see that," I said, turning to face her at the wooden picnic table a few feet away from where our children and Roger were playing. Ursula had a very defined jaw line. I watched as she twirled her long, blonde hair around her fingers, creating soft waves that fell on her bare shoulders. She was wearing a short pink and white dress, with spaghetti straps that exposed her very tanned skin. I silently wondered how much money she spent at the tanning salon to achieve that look.

"We are very family-oriented people," she continued. "Our children go to the best schools and we spend a lot of time together. We also go to church every week and we work very hard to give our children the best things in life. I know we have three children already and you must be wondering why we'd want another."

"The thought crossed my mind."

"Well, I have never been able to get pregnant naturally." She looked down at her hands as if she were ashamed of this. "I carried all the children, but they were all born very early. The last pregnancy, with the twins... well it was very dangerous for all of us. I was on hospital bed-rest from eighteen weeks until they were born at twenty-eight weeks. It was necessary to keep them in long enough for them to survive. Being born that early affects them on a daily basis. You may not be able to see it right away, but it's something we struggle with every moment of every day."

"That must have been terrible," I said quietly.

"The doctors told me it wouldn't be safe for me to carry again. We still have two embryos, though," she said, turning her gaze towards me. "The clinic says that the embryos are really only good for about five years. We're reaching that point very quickly and we can't afford to keep them in storage for any longer than that. Besides, we feel that if we don't use them now, we never will.

"I don't feel like my family is complete," she went on. "I mean, if we try and we fail, then at least we can say we tried. But if we don't try, then it's like throwing away those two babies. They are my babies. I can't just throw them away."

I did not say anything at first, staying quiet as I tried to put myself in her position. She was a mother with so many blessings, and yet having those two possible souls sitting in a freezer somewhere, waiting patiently for someone to decide whether or not to give them a chance at life, clearly disturbed her greatly. If the only options were to give the embryos a chance or not to give them a chance, then there was not really any other decision than to try.

Roger came towards us, leaving the kids to play by themselves in the playground. "You two getting along?" he asked, taking a seat next to Ursula. Roger was slightly shorter than Ursula and almost as thin. His aviator sunglasses rested on his long, narrow nose and he smoothed back his brown hair with the palms of his hands.

"Perfectly," I said. "We were just talking about your children."

Ursula smiled at Roger. "I told Crystal about how special our children are to us, and how we'd like to have another child without having to worry about prematurity."

I could tell that Ursula had a harder time than Roger with the decision of whether or not to use the embryos. I could see in her eyes that she longed to be able to carry again but the doctors' orders had been clear. They would not implant any more embryos into her after what she had already experienced.

Ursula shifted in her seat as she spoke about their lives and twirled her hair when she mentioned the twins. Her body language told me she felt deep sadness for her son and daughter. She often looked away, her eyes turning glassy as she held back her tears.

Roger grabbed Ursula's hand and kissed it gently. "This is something she has been begging me to do since the children were very small. We really feel that the time is now."

When I made the decision to become a surrogate I wanted it to be for someone who did not have any children—someone who had never felt a baby kick from inside; a woman who had never experienced the pain of labor or the joy of a newly born baby. But sitting across from me, here was a couple who had not got what they wanted for their family either. They had three beautiful children but my heart ached for Ursula, knowing the seriousness of the predicament her earlier pregnancies had caused her.

We said our goodbyes and I waved to them as they got into their SUV and drove away. Neither Roger nor Ursula asked how I felt about carrying their babies for them and I was thankful for that. I needed a little time to process my thoughts.

I grabbed Anne and Emmy and hoisted them into my

CHAPTER SEVEN

double jogging stroller. Even though it was almost August, the setting of the sun brought cooler temperatures and a soft breeze sent the smell of summer's wildflowers across my face. I have always felt that the freshness of the night can bring the most enlightenment when it comes to problems that need to be solved and questions that need answers.

It was starting to get dark, and my girls were both snuggled half-asleep in the stroller. As I looked at them, I thought about what it would be like to know that they had a brother or sister, maybe even two, who were not yet introduced into the world. Even worse, what it would be like to be faced with the possibility of needing to thaw and discard them as if they were nothing.

I understood the urgency Roger and Ursula felt. They needed someone who could carry, and soon. Since most of my tests had already been completed, it seemed as if I was meant to help them. Having identified themselves as Catholics, their faith was obviously something important to them. Ursula spoke about the embryos as if they were already living breathing children; she felt that they were babies and not merely clumps of cells or tissue that could be easily dispensed with. At the same time, watching them interact with their children assured me that they could provide a good home for any additional children they might have. With the educational and financial benefits only a stable and high income household could provide, their children had a bright future ahead of them. They spoke of an addition to the family as if it had already been decided. I could see that they, Ursula especially, were anticipating bringing another life into their family with welcome arms and plenty of resources. Their children would never struggle.

As I approached my house, I noticed that Anne and Emmy were now both sound asleep. I parked the stroller in the driveway and carried them one by one into the house. Scott was not home yet and the house was dark and quiet.

It was a clear night. From my front porch I could see millions of tiny bright stars in the sky. The moon was almost full, a bright golden globe that drew me into its beauty. I stared up at it, thinking about the new life I could bring to Roger and Ursula.

I had come to a decision.

After a few moments I walked into the house to send my answer to Sharon.

CHAPTER SEVEN

A great soul
will be strong
to live as
well as think.

—Ralph Waldo
Emerson

CHAPTER EIGHT
September 2, 2011

The contract Sharon sent me looked just like the first draft of the one I had signed with Mark. I wondered if it was a standard contract she used for all her clients, impersonal to the new situation with Roger and Ursula.

As I was about to save the attachment to my desktop, I saw another email coming in from Sharon:

Crystal,

Since this contract was already finalized, why don't we just use it again? We'll change all the contact information. Roger and Ursula are calling the clinic now to see what they need you to

do, but this will move quickly, so we should get this finalized
as soon as possible. Let me know if there is anything else you
would like changed.

Sharon

I read through it again and noticed there were some things
that seemed questionable. Sharon had not adjusted any of the
wording to indicate that Roger and Ursula were now the intended
parents rather than Mark, a single man, and as I glanced through
each line of the document, I fought the urge to correct her spelling
and grammatical errors.

After a discussion I'd had with another surrogate, I decided
to increase the amount of my life insurance, and the fee if I lost the
use of any of my reproductive organs. I knew I didn't want any more
children right away but I wanted to have the option should I change
my mind in the future. There was always the chance that something
could go wrong with the surrogacy pregnancy and I could lose my
reproductive ability.

Other features, such as the addition of a bed-rest stipend,
and childcare for when I attended doctors' appointments, were also
important, so I certainly needed to add those items into the contract.

With Mark, I had been so sure of everything I committed
to and I really didn't take my time reading the second draft.
However, I did notice the termination clause and this time
I decided to say something about it. In Mark's case I knew
he was willing to accept as many babies as the number of
embryos implanted, but I wasn't comfortable making that
same assumption for the Stones. I wished we had talked more
about their views on termination, but when I thought about the
previous conversations we had, I was fairly certain I knew their

feelings on the matter. I had originally wanted to change that part of the contract to say that I would only agree to terminate if the child was not going to live, or if the pregnancy was going to result in serious detriment of health to myself, so before I sent the email back to Sharon asking her for the additions, I added a quick note at the bottom about the termination clause.

> Sharon,
>
> I'm not really comfortable with the termination clause as it is stated currently. I am not willing to consider termination unless the child is going to die or if it puts me in serious jeopardy. Can you please revise the phrasing to reflect this?
>
> Thanks,
> Crystal

A few hours later I received a revised version of the contract.

> Ursula and Crystal,
>
> I incorporated the changes each of you asked about.
>
> Please review and let me know if you need to add, remove, or change anything.
>
> Sharon

I read over the changes that had been made. The clause had previously stated:

> Gestational carrier agrees to selective fetus reduction and/or abortion at the discretion of the Intended Parent.

Abortion and selective reduction due to severe fetus
abnormality:

The Gestational Carrier agrees to selective fetus reduction or/
and abortion in case of severe fetus abnormality as determined
by 3-dimensional ultrasound test with following pathology
expertise, or by any other procedure or test(s) used to diagnose
severe fetus abnormality.

The words 'severe fetus abnormality' stuck out for me. They
left a lot of unanswered questions, such as who would determine
what was thought to be severe? How severe was severe enough?
What would happen, and when? The term was ambiguous and
vague. I thought about having Sharon change it again, but when I
emailed her back to ask if there was any more room for changes, I
was told that we did not want to squander precious time trying to
alter the contract and that it was a standard clause used all the time. I
had a day or so to approve the contract or risk the possibility of losing
the match due to the quickly approaching deadline for the embryos.

That night as I lay in bed, I thought about the clause. I
couldn't decide how I would amend it if I were to rewrite the
contract. I was not sure if I should even bother. I did not want to
appear to be too picky and therefore be perceived to be difficult.
I also did not want to put myself in a bad position. My biggest
concern was that the pregnancy might affect my ability to have
more children. I didn't ever want to be placed in the predicament
the Stones were in if I could help it. I also didn't want to make
things arduous, but I definitely could not agree to termination for
just any reason.

I pulled the covers over my shoulders, shutting out the world. I tried to escape the words of Ursula Stone that played over and over in my head, but my thoughts kept returning to them. *'They are my babies, I can't just throw them away.'*

Her statement led me to believe she was someone who would accept a child with Down's Syndrome or any other genetic problem that happened to subsume their lives. Roger and Ursula said they were Catholics and seemed fairly religious, going to church every week. Since the Catholic Church has a public stance against abortion, I believed their faith was strong enough to hold them true to those values. And the fact that I had never heard of a surrogate being asked to abort a fetus led me to accept the contract written the way it was. I believed the chances were extremely slim that anything would happen to cause a problem, since I also had loving parents with a pro-life stance behind me.

THREE DAYS EARLIER

"Ms. Kelley? I need to speak with you please."

Looking longingly out the front door I picked myself up out of my chair and walked over to the receptionist desk. It was such a beautiful day. I wished I was sitting outside instead of waiting in the doctor's practice to talk to a man who would go over my entire medical file to see if I was fit to carry another child.

"Yes, what is it?" I asked, leaning over to match the receptionist's hushed voice.

"Mrs. Stone is on the phone. She wants to know if you are here. Am I allowed to tell her that you are?"

"Oh, of course."

Smiling at the attractive receptionist, I laughed to myself. Ursula had begged the clinic to forego their usual practice of meeting with potential surrogates and asked them to approve me for the procedure without that little formality. She had told me numerous times that they had no doubts about their match and that they wanted to get everything else out of the way so that we could move quickly to the cycle. They had even pushed up the procedure by a month. However, it was still important that I became comfortable with the doctor who would eventually perform the embryo transfer.

His name was difficult to pronounce and he had a heavy accent. Luckily I had lived in several different cultural environments, so within a short time I was able to understand him fairly well. His office was one of the corner spaces, enclosed in glass with a couple of short walls painted a soft yellow. African tribal masks decorated the room and an ebony elephant rested on a tall, cherry shelf. The desk below the shelf was covered in files and textbooks. It almost looked like he had just moved in, with books piled everywhere and eclectic trinkets scattered throughout the office. It wasn't anything like I had imagined from the write-up in the brochure I had read in the waiting room, stating that he had been in residence with the clinic for over a decade.

He motioned for me to sit down opposite him in an oversized red leather chair. As he looked through my file he glanced at me over the rim of his thin gold glasses. I could feel judgment shooting like lasers across his large oak desk from his eyes to mine.

"Tell me about your previous pregnancies," he said, looking up at me with his hands folded on the file.

I knew he was talking about the babies I had lost, but I did not want to start on a negative note, so I talked first about my living children. I explained Anne's heart defect, citing a source that had determined her particular defect to have little to no basis in genetics, then went on to describe my second pregnancy with Emmy.

"And the other pregnancies?"

"They were years ago. I was very young and they were close together. Many years passed before I became pregnant with my oldest child. I've had no problems carrying since then. Both my children were born full term and are very healthy."

The doctor sat back. He touched his index finger to his lips and sighed. "Okay."

We talked some more about my medical history, my asthma, and the bout I'd had with postpartum depression.

"Do you feel it's managed now?"

"Oh yes. I didn't have any depressive symptoms after my second child. I attribute that to a conscious decision we made as a family to be more healthy. We eat an organic diet and use as few toxins as possible in our everyday lives. I have not been on any medication for depression or anxiety in over five years now, and I keep up with maintenance on my mental health to be able to recognize if and when there is a breakdown so that it can be caught early and handled appropriately."

He turned his head, staring towards the wall of masks to his left. After what seemed like hours he closed the file. Looking back at me, he removed his glasses. "Well, I don't know what I would say to you if you were applying for our in-house surrogacy program, but we do like to try to take the directives of the agency when we are dealing with outside firms, and you are who the Stones want to use. I'll need a psychological evaluation and a mock transfer but you'll be fine to carry."

His statement surprised me. Contracts still had not been

signed and I was fairly sure that the meet and greet at the clinic had been something that needed to happen for the clinic to agree to use me. But I did not question it. The other clinic had done things a little differently but there had been no initial interview required, unlike what had just occurred. It was all so confusing but Sharon warned me that different clinics had different policies.

Sharon tried to circumvent the psychological evaluation, telling me it was unnecessary. She said she could see that I was appropriately pursuing surrogacy and had a healthy attitude towards it. My counselor agreed with that assertion, so Sharon decided she would perform this part of the process. Since she was licensed as a social worker in New York, I thought her expertise would be enough to elicit a reputable opinion and allow us to move forward. So far there wasn't a single person who had ever said I did not go into surrogacy without the proper expectations, ideals, and emotional stability.

The all-important phone conversation with Sharon took place as I was standing in the courtyard of Paul Revere's famous house in Boston. A friend had come to the area for the week so Anne, Emmy and I went to meet her. Boston is a short train ride from where we lived, so trips like this were not too much of a hassle, even if they were not cheap. It was something we had only done once before so I was not about to pass up a chance to get together with an old friend, especially after Sharon told me we could talk over the phone rather than in person.

I walked around the fountain outside while my girls sat on a nearby bench and ate eclairs with my friend and her two children. A few passers-by looked over at me when they saw me on the phone, furrowing their brows as Sharon and I talked about very personal information. After a while I retreated to one of the enclosed gardens, needing to be alone when a particularly sensitive topic came up. I found a corner where I could still see the girls, laughing and running around the fountain, chasing each other and splashing one another with the water.

About a half hour later, the interview was complete. Sharon told me she would write up her report and let them know that I was psychologically approved.

"This is going to be great," she said.

One word
frees us of
all the weight
and pain of life:
That word is
love.

—Sophocles

CHAPTER NINE
August 24, 2011

The day my first package of medications arrived a
wave of panic struck me out of nowhere. Everything
had been so rushed and I didn't have a moment to think about
another cycle or the embryo transfer. I sat down at my kitchen table,
staring out the window, hoping I had made the right choice to start
all over again with a new couple.

I opened the box and found the first shot. Removing its plastic
wrapping, I stared at the long needle I had to stick into my body. I
took a deep breath, pinched the skin of my thigh together, cringing
as the needle released a wave of hormones into my body. I pulled my
sweatpants back up to my waist and rubbed the injection site, willing
the pain away.

■ ■ ■

I started the cycle for the second time before the latest contract was even signed. We were supposed to meet as a group and sign the contract together but were not able to make our schedules work out. After a few weeks of taking the medication, all parties had put ink to paper, binding us as partners through the surrogacy.

I knew the first two weeks would go smoothly since I had already completed that part of the cycle before. It was the later weeks I was worried about. The clinic insisted upon prescribing progesterone shots for pregnancy maintenance if the transfer worked. I was having some difficulty with the small needles for the Lupron, never mind the big fat needles they used to do Progesterone shots. My hands shook every time I administered the Lupron through my own skin. I didn't know how I would bear the larger needles for Progesterone.

We searched for a few days for a nurse who would travel to me to inject those shots but never found anyone. With a good deal of pressure, finally the clinic changed the prescription to enable me to use suppositories instead.

As the weeks went on, giving myself the Lupron shots got easier and easier. I learned how to grasp my skin so that I barely felt the pinch. Although I changed injection sites almost daily, my upper thighs would ache all day long, making sitting for extended periods of time a very difficult task. Unfortunately, the regimen for the lab work and ultrasounds I needed to determine the time of transfer required me to travel all over the state. I spent a lot of time in my car, rubbing my legs with one hand while the other gripped the steering wheel.

I also often needed blood tests but that lab was near my

home. By my third visit my forearms began to turn a bright shade of purple, matching the beautiful shade of blue on my thighs. I quickly became friendly with the nurses there, who asked how the process was going every time I saw them, and I actually began to look forward to those appointments. Many other days I drove to New Britain's fertility clinic for ultrasounds. They needed to monitor the lining of my uterus to decide when would be the most ideal moment to transfer the embryos. Unfortunately, they could not perform remote monitoring like other facilities did, so I had to drive forty-five minutes away for those appointments. I dreaded traveling back and forth to the facility after Scott came home from work but also enjoyed the time to myself. Each time I had to go to New Britain, I would park a short distance away from the entrance and take a relaxing walk before I went inside, then another walk after I got out. It was nice to spend the cooler end-of-summer evenings outside with the breeze at my back, rather than always being stuck in the house with little voices in my ears and hands in my pockets.

■ ■ ■

Shortly into the cycling phase, I started feeling very angry and suspicious of Scott's behavior. The influence of the fertility drugs made my moods change drastically. I found myself arguing with almost everyone around me. Sometimes it would be the kids who got on my nerves and other times it was Scott.

"I can't stand the way you are lately," he shouted at me.

"Then leave," I yelled back.

The tension between us became too much for him to deal with and he eventually left the house, slamming the door behind him without even glancing back.

Anne and Emmy were fast asleep and thankfully didn't hear any part of our conversation, or so I hoped. I sat on the couch in the living room, sobbing in between fits of anger.

"Fine!" I shrieked into the air. "Go! See if I care."

I spent the next few days in a tyranny of indignation and sadness. I didn't know what to do with myself or how I would take care of the girls. I was furious with Scott for the injustice I perceived and could not see a way to forgive him for his behavior. To me, breaking up was the only option. Until Scott was ready to declare his dedication to our family, I couldn't have him in my life.

Without the financial help Scott provided, I would need to figure out how to support the three of us. I had been a stay-at-home mother and nanny for so long that I did not even know where to start looking for another job. My life was defined by my children but I knew I had to figure out how to make things work on my own.

My new adventure as a surrogate didn't allow for much free time to find another job. Between all the appointments and the possibility that I might end up carrying a child in the near future, I wasn't sure how I would squeeze in another career. Plus, where would we live if we didn't live with Scott?

I asked the landlord to extend the date our rent was due to enable me to save a little more money to pay for it, but he wasn't willing to allow that so we all had to leave. In the few days after we ended our relationship, Scott had found a new place and said he could keep the kids while I searched for another home. Of course, that meant I would have to stay with him as well; he worked from early in the morning until late at night, so I would have to take care of Emmy and Anne anyway.

We packed our things, piling boxes and toys into my tiny car before driving over to Scott's new house where we could temporarily settle down as the dysfunctional family we had come to be.

■　■　■

Little by little life had let me down. It was a feeling I knew well, and it weighed heavily on me. As much as I hated it, I needed to find something to keep myself out of the dismal abyss before me. I concentrated on the surrogacy and forced myself to think positively about the future and of my future baby's life, when I didn't even know there was a baby yet. The idea that I would be bringing a new life into the hands of a family who would care for and mold that life into something wonderful made my darkest days brighter. My partnership with Roger and Ursula would also give me enough financial security to pay bills and support the girls on my own. I was going to have to work extra hard to save towards using the financial benefit of surrogacy for my business but I was sure I could utilize my time during the pregnancy to get the necessary certifications and set things up so that, once my time as a surrogate was over, the business would be workable.

I felt very guilty relying on the situation with Roger and Ursula for financial support. That was never what I had intended to do. I wanted to be able to provide for my children without that, and create my business solely with the money I earned as a surrogate. However, life had led me on a different path before, and without Scott that was no longer possible.

Yet every time I thought of Ursula and her desire for her family I envisioned a happy ending, one filled with excitement over the child we had created together. I had been on the other end of her struggle and understood that nothing should be taken for granted.

I knew the feelings she was experiencing, and even more so, I knew what it would feel like if I were to back out now. I had dealt with disappointment in my own life and I didn't want to be the source of distress for anyone else. I wanted the happy ending with a happy family, and a lifelong connection. I needed to make sure I kept my focus on the task at hand, blocking every depressive thought from my mind. Anne and Emmy deserved a mom who was focused and pleasant to be around.

I never did pick up the phone to tell Sharon that Scott had moved out. I guess I just did not feel it affected what I intended to do. I still wanted to have a baby for the Stones. I didn't want a baby for myself, especially then, but I wanted something to give me hope.

What better to symbolize hope than a new life?

> We do the best
> that we can;
> we never know
> what miracle is
> wrought in our
> life, or in the life
> of another.
>
> —Helen Keller

CHAPTER TEN
October 5, 2011

Scott had come with me on this 'crazy journey,' as he called it. We had been talking a lot during the previous two weeks, and while we were still a long way from okay, we were civil. He was still concerned about my welfare through the surrogacy process. I was not allowed to drive myself home from this insemination procedure, so Scott agreed to come even though I was sure he did not really want to be there.

We'd had a pleasant evening the night before, driving up from Connecticut and staying in a hotel room secured by Ursula and Roger. In the morning Scott was the one who reminded me to drink a pitcher of water per the clinic's recommendation. I had received paperwork in the mail with the directions for the day of insemination that instructed me to have a full bladder so that the catheterization process would go smoothly. I desperately needed to use the bathroom but was sure they would not allow me to do so. I tried to relax, laying my hands over my belly but quickly removing them, the slightest pressure making me feel as though I would burst.

The receptionist asked if 'the other couple' was coming. I knew Ursula and Roger wanted to come to the insemination but Roger could not miss work and Ursula was home with their oldest child who had caught a stomach bug that had infected half their town. She called me on my way while Scott and I were in the car. I did not pick up but listened to her voice message as she wished me well. Her words told me she was just as anxious as I was. A quick look at my Facebook page told me that a lot of my friends and other surrogates I had met during the matching process were all rooting for me, too.

While I sat down, Scott immediately turned to the pile of magazines. Several nurses passed by and I wondered if they knew I was a surrogate. Did they recognize every infertile couple who came to them for help, from those of us who were surrogates? Was there any way to tell the difference? Since I was perfectly capable of creating life without medical help, it felt strange to enter through the same doors that so many infertile couples passed through with only a hope for a baby to sustain them.

This was the big day; the past month littered with preparation could all be for nothing, dispelling the calm I had forced myself into as we sat, once again waiting. I glanced around at the other patients, eager for anything to distract me from my swelling bladder.

At the other end of the long L-shaped room, a young couple,

immersed in paperwork, exchanged nervous looks. The woman kept gazing around while she flipped through the documents, her hands shaking as she scanned page after page. I turned towards the receptionist who was hard at work, often leaving the desk for several minutes before returning to use the phone or file medical information away in the large cabinets behind her. Every time I wanted to get up to ask her when we'd be seen, she would vanish to the back of the office.

"You sure you want to do this?" Scott asked. "You can still back out if you want to."

"Thanks, but I do really want to be here," I replied, tapping my fingertips on the wooden arm of the chair and biting my nails on my other hand.

He shrugged and went back to reading the magazine.

Moments later a nurse called my name and led me to a narrow room that was designed like the locker rooms you see at the gym. There were about eight metal lockers lining one wall, a bench, and a few bathroom stalls. I asked the nurse if I could use the bathroom but she insisted I wait until after the procedure. When I told her the choice was to urinate or lose control of my bladder, probably on the doctor, she agreed that I could use the restroom. I was instructed to try to empty only half of the contents of my bladder but I could not stop halfway through. The release felt so satisfying but I hoped it wouldn't affect the procedure.

The nurse gave me a paper gown and a plastic hair cap to put on. "For sterility purposes," she said.

She left me alone to change and I placed all my clothes and my purse in one of the lockers. She came back a few minutes later and led me down a long hallway to a small nurses' station. About halfway down the hall I could see a round table and a desk with a stack of paperwork on it, and at the end I could see the doctor staring down at his laptop. The nurses asked me to sign the final consent paperwork before leading me into the procedure room.

The room was like an examining room, only bigger. The examination table sat in the middle of the room, and just as they were at the obstetrician's clinic, the stirrups were already out and awaiting their next occupant. When I sat down, the nurse explained how the doctor would want me positioned and how the procedure would go.

"When the doctor is done, we'll leave you in here for about twenty minutes to let the embryos settle. We ask that you lie still and not move around too much."

I smiled back at her and thought it would be nice if this experience were more personal. Not that I needed a lounge chair and low lighting, but it all seemed so *clinical*. My experience of making babies up until this point involved lots of touching and a nice soft bed, not cold, metallic equipment and strangers telling me to take my clothes off.

It was chilly in the room and yet I knew I would be expected to bare all and expose myself for an unmeasured amount of time awaiting the doctor, the embryos, and the twenty minutes afterwards.

I hopped up onto the table, making a crisp, crunching sound as I plopped down onto the protective white paper covering. I was in there for quite a while by myself before there was a quiet knock and the doctor appeared in the doorway.

"Ms. Kelley, a pleasure to see you again," he said, extending his hand to me.

"Yes, you too."

"I've been to the thawing chamber and have seen the

embryos today. It looks as though they are both doing well and ready for transfer. What we're going to do today won't take any time at all. It will be just like the mock transfer you had at home, only this time we'll do some waiting afterwards so that we can look under the microscope at the catheter and confirm that both embryos have moved into the uterine cavity. Afterwards, I'd like you to remain lying down for twenty minutes to give your body time to rest." He tapped his pen on his clipboard, then put the end into his mouth, biting it gently. "In my experience most women come in here very tense so it helps to relax once insemination has occurred. Sound okay?"

"That sounds good. Yes." I placed my heels in the stirrups and let out a deep sigh.

"Just relax," the doctor said. "The hardest part of this whole thing is the waiting."

The doctor was very tall, and when he sat down on the round, rolling chair, he had to arch his back downward to get a good view of the space between my legs.

"You're going to feel some pressure from the speculum and then I'll insert the catheter. You may feel a bit uncomfortable but it will only be in for a few seconds."

Much like the many routine trips to the gynecologist I've had since I was a teenager, the worst part was over in a few moments. The mock trial had been very uncomfortable, even painful, but with this doctor the procedure was quick, painless, and I almost didn't know it was happening until it was over. We had to wait a few minutes for one of the nurses to confirm that the embryos were indeed not stuck and had moved from the catheter. Once they did that, it was over.

The nurse gave me a sheet to lay over my lower half and

instructed me not to get up and put on my clothes until the twenty minutes had passed. At that moment I wished I had grabbed one of the magazines from the waiting room.

As the doctor and nurse left the room, the door shut slowly behind them, leaving me to ponder what I had just done. I visualized the two little babies inside my belly as they found a comfortable spot in my uterine lining, imagining it being like two little baby bears during a long winter nap who find comfort in the folds of their mother's thick fur.

Some people thought I was making the ultimate sacrifice by having a baby for someone else, making me fat and hormonal for the next nine months for people I didn't even know. But I did not see it that way.

I stared at the ceiling. For me, pregnancy was never hard. I enjoyed every second when I carried Anne and Emmy. I expected this pregnancy to be no different.

With a small smile on my face I was lost in thought when there was another knock on the door. The nurse came in carrying a handful of paperwork.

"All right," she said. "Time's up. You can get dressed. I'll meet you outside this room and walk you out."

As I stood up, I felt a rush of blood to my head and realized I had not eaten all day. It was clinic policy to come with an empty stomach but it was now almost noon and I was starving. I quickly put on my clothes and walked out the door. As we headed back to the locker room the nurse chatted to me about what to look for, like the wait time for pregnancy testing. I tried to concentrate on her instructions but also found myself clenching my rear end in an attempt to keep the babies inside and secure. I felt like I had to keep my pelvic floor muscles tight even though I knew what I was doing probably wouldn't help and only made my walk a bit awkward.

"So, how'd it go?" Scott asked, standing up to greet me.

"Fine. Quicker than I expected."

"Good. When will you know if it worked?"

"I'll have a blood test in ten days and an ultrasound after that."

"You have to wait almost two weeks? Damn!"

"I know. I wish I could take it sooner. Listen, I'm going to call Ursula and let her know how it went. I'll meet you in the car."

"Okay."

Ursula answered on the first ring, her phone most likely by her side all day as she waited anxiously for my call.

"Hey, Ursula. I wanted to let you know that it's all done. It was easy and I'm on my way home now."

"Oh my goodness that's so wonderful! Do you feel pregnant?"

I chuckled. "I think it's a little early to tell."

"All right. Well, drive safely home. We'll talk to you soon."

■　■　■

The ride home was just as long but there was a lot less conversation this time. We were both tired from the journey the night before and waking up early so we could make the appointment at the clinic. While Scott drove, I stared out the passenger window, frantically trying to remember all the things the nurse had told me to do to increase the chances of retaining at least one of the embryos. For most of the ride I put my feet up on the dashboard and leaned as far back in my seat as I could. It seemed like a really long time to be stuck in the same position, but I was scared to sit up; I felt that the fate of these little babies depended on my ability to keep them safe in my uterus and not let them fall out.

As we made the long trek home I dozed on and off, dreaming about the tiny embryos growing inside me.

OCTOBER 14, 2011

They had not told me to take a test before the blood work began, but I was so anxious and excited at the prospect of being pregnant that I couldn't help it: I went to the local pharmacy on day six, post-transfer, and bought a three-pack of pregnancy tests.

I put them under the sink in the bathroom at Scott's house, where I would be less tempted to use them. I had the appointment scheduled with the lab on Friday morning, but I was not sure how long it would take for the results to come in.

By Tuesday I was driving myself crazy. I began to experience what I can only describe as phantom symptoms of pregnancy that would come and go. My breasts would be tender for a day and then feel fine. I felt bloated, and then I felt nauseous. A few hours later I would be full of energy and ravenous but unable to eat.

Tuesday night I decided to take one of the tests. I knew that a late day test would be less accurate but I had three tests, so I figured it wouldn't hurt to use one.

In between episodes of our favorite show on Netflix, I snuck off to the bathroom. Too nervous to wait there and watch, I left the test on the counter for a few minutes before going back to it during the next commercial break.

There was nothing on the test screen.

"What if it didn't work?" I asked Scott.

He looked at me blankly. I'm sure he didn't know what to say and I really did not expect an answer anyway. I tried hard to quell my nervous feelings and decided to turn in for the night. Since we were waiting to move into our new house, Scott was letting us stay with him for a few weeks. It was nice to have him around but I was still unsure of what to do about the relationship so I didn't dare share too much or try to provoke conversation. That night, though, I wanted some reassurance. Before I headed for the bedroom Scott tried to put his arm around me, and for the first time since we had broken up, I let him.

"Whatever is meant to happen will happen," he said in a voice full of gentleness.

I laughed, since Scott had just said what I always say to friends when I'm at a loss for words of advice.

I woke up several times during the night. I wanted to know for sure, and kept checking the clock, wondering if it was too early to take the other test. At seven a.m. Scott got up and went to work. I brought Emmy into bed with me and tried to will my mind to relax. By nine a.m., I was awake and pacing with anticipation. I hadn't used the bathroom yet and knew I couldn't step onto the cold tile floor without reaching for the second test.

As I placed the white stick back on the sink to wait for the results, I closed my eyes. I kept them closed and walked out of the room. The girls were up, making a mess in the kitchen, Scott's pots and pans strewn across the floor. For a moment I got lost in motherly chores, cleaning up spilled cereal, pouring juice, and setting out clothes for the day. Fifteen minutes passed before I had a moment to check the results.

For a brief second I stood outside the bathroom door, reminding myself that we only had one shot at this. If it didn't work, then it was not meant to be.

I opened the door.

The room was dark and for a moment I groped around on the wall before finding the light switch.

Once my eyes adjusted I saw it, Stormie.

Two pink lines.

> All who think cannot but see there is a sanction like that of religion which binds us in partnership in the serious work of the world.
>
> —Benjamin Franklin

CHAPTER ELEVEN
October 18, 2011

"**I**t worked! You're pregnant!" Ursula said, her voice reaching a decibel only audible to our four-legged canine friends.

"I told you I wasn't joking." I said. "When did they call you?"

"A few minutes ago. We're both really excited. Thank you so much, Crystal."

The phone call was almost a joke to me. I had called Ursula the same morning I took the pregnancy test; the same morning I saw the two pink lines. You were there, Stormie. She hadn't believed the results, stating that she wanted to wait for the official blood test which was two days later. So for two whole days I carried the news around, guarding my secret from anyone else. I only told the people who were involved in my life every day—Scott, Lisette, and my mom and dad. I even kept it quiet on Facebook, despite the anticipation and questions from friends.

"Sure. I'm glad it worked right away. The ultrasound will be scheduled in a couple of weeks. I'll let you know when it is, all right?"

"Yes, of course. We'd love to come to that ultrasound if we can. We want to be as involved as possible."

"In the meantime, Ursula, have we heard anything about the insurance from Sharon? I'm going to have to go to the doctor soon to transfer care."

"I'll call Sharon and see where that stands. I agree we should get you to the doctor's as soon as possible. Can you call and schedule an appointment now?"

"Absolutely."

■　■　■

I had left the kids in the house with Scott, giving me a few moments of alone-time in the car before I ventured inside. It was close to the end of October. The weathermen were predicting very cold weather for the coming days, but I enjoyed the fifty-degree temperatures I breathed in from the open side window.

As I sat in my car I thought about how the journey had gone so far. Things had been complicated, to say the least, but they had gone well and now, Stormie, we had the exciting confirmation that I was indeed pregnant with you. I just hoped that the next chapter of the process would go as favorably.

The quest to pregnancy had been what I worried about most, and I didn't really see any further complications on the horizon. However, it was essential to get past the danger zone in the first few weeks, when I needed the progesterone to maintain the pregnancy. The doctors had told me I could start weaning off the progesterone around nine or ten weeks into gestation, or one week after the first ultrasound. In the meantime, now was the time when Sharon had said we would get all the insurances and necessities set up.

I had a $300,000 life insurance policy as well as health insurance built into my contract. I knew we would have to go elsewhere for the health insurance but for the life insurance I wanted to deal with people I already knew. Nadia, the agent I had previously worked with for car insurance, had become a good friend of mine and I knew she would never steer me wrong.

I called her, explaining the situation as best I could while she described my options. She gave me a price and I asked her to email Ursula and explicate the policy, giving her the yearly cost. I figured it would be easier if they paid it all at once, since the amount was minute in comparison to some of the other things they had already purchased.

"All right, then," I said. "Now we just need to figure out the health insurance."

"What do you mean?" Nadia asked. "You don't have insurance already?"

"No, I'm covered by Medicaid and all the IVF fees were paid for out-of-pocket. I was told not to worry about the insurance and that it would be taken care of."

"Well, I really hope they did something ahead of time for you, Crystal," she said. "If you aren't covered now, you're likely to be denied any coverage that you apply for. Pregnancy is considered a pre-existing condition and most insurance companies in Connecticut won't cover you if you haven't already had their coverage for a period of time before the conception date."

"What? No one's ever told me that before."

I hung up and called Sharon to confirm.

"Oh, don't worry about that," she said. "We don't mention the pregnancy in the beginning. It's as if you find out about it after coverage has begun. I've never had a problem doing it this way."

Her answer sounded ethically wrong, but at that point I didn't think there was much I could do about it. If I was going to get insurance coverage I had to go along with what she had planned. She sent me the paperwork and told me, "Just don't tell them you're pregnant yet."

I filled it out quickly and sent it in before I could let the feeling that I was doing something wrong settle into my stomach. It turned out it didn't matter because I was denied coverage anyway, but it was weeks before I received any notification that I was denied, and after I sent the papers in I had a very bad feeling in the pit of my stomach. I attributed it mostly to the pregnancy and tried to forget that the documents I had just sent in were falsified.

■　■　■

It was a beautiful time of year, warmer than I remembered most October months, until one night it got bitterly cold and started snowing. Snowstorm Alfred buried us under almost four feet of snow and ice. For over a week power in our little town was out, and during that time we lost everything in our refrigerator, including the progesterone I had been using several times a day.

Stormie, I worried so much that I would lose you as a result of that. Every night, as I rubbed my stomach with the palms of my hands in a circular motion and looked up toward the ceiling, I would repeat my personal positivity:

"Please stay with me, little one. Please make it till the end."

You will never know, Stormie, how much I hoped it would work.

■ ■ ■

By the time the power was restored, it was time for me to move. We were scheduled to relocate to our new house on November first and I couldn't wait to have a place to call my own. While I organized our new two bedroom apartment, Scott made dinner then watched cartoons with Anne and Emmy. I was unpacking the silverware for the kitchen when I heard giggling coming from the living room. I glanced around the corner to the room filled with boxes and saw the girls cuddled with Scott on the couch, laughing as he tickled them. Seeing them interact together made me smile but I also felt sad, thinking about how it would be so much nicer if things were back to the way they had once been with Scott when we first met. I missed having a companion and I wanted my girls to have their father.

But, strangely enough, since Scott and I had separated we had spent very little time actually living apart. He was still a big part of my support system and acted remorsefully for the way he had behaved when he caused our breakup. I still wasn't sure I could trust him, or that I wanted him around, but I did want to make sure he remained a big part of our lives. It would not be fair to cut him out of our lives completely. Anne and Emmy needed their father and I would not stand in the way of that.

■ ■ ■

CHAPTER ELEVEN

Shortly after moving I got a call from my doctor's office. They were still awaiting insurance information in order to bill the cost of the clinic visits and the care I would receive. Since I had heard nothing at that time about the status of my insurance, I called Sharon. She told me to email the insurance company, and when I did, I received notification that I had been denied. I still don't know how or why I was denied, but deep down I was relieved that I didn't have to worry about them finding out I had been pregnant when I applied, possibly dropping my coverage or coming after me for fraudulent use of the service. On the other hand, this was now a problem. The obstetrician's practice I was planning to use charged a minimum of $500 per visit. This wasn't something Ursula and Roger were financially prepared for, or so they explained to me.

I was scheduled to have my first doctor's visit around ten weeks, shortly after the first ultrasound. When the ultrasound came and went and we still hadn't figured out how to manage the costs, I had to realize the possibility that I would not be able to use my own doctor for this pregnancy. The clinic I had named in the contract was the same one I had used during the pregnancy and subsequent delivery of my youngest daughter. It was a practice that really gave importance to patient care and was supportive of natural birth. I had switched to their practice after the birth of my first daughter, and was much happier with their care and the hospital in which they operated. I pleaded with the practice manager to work with Ursula and Roger to come up with a payment plan so that I could utilize them again.

Ultimately, they were unable to come to any agreement, and we needed to find other options. The state's insurance was a possibility, but it was over $400 per month, and when speaking to the representative at the social services office about it, she told me I wouldn't qualify anyway since it was not intended for surrogacy cases.

It looked as though we were out of options.

Being a doula, however, I had other resources at my disposal. I asked our regional forum about alternatives, and was referred to several home birth midwives, and also one birth center in Danbury, Connecticut. It was the only birth center in the state and I knew that would be our last option.

Ursula and Roger had never known pregnancy and birth to be anything other than a medical event, and although I was only concerned about my personal ability to birth without an epidural, I doubted they would be open to the idea of a home birth. I called the birth center and explained the situation as best I could without mentioning I was a surrogate. Ursula had asked me to keep that information private. She feared it would change the way we were viewed, and therefore treated. We scheduled a walk-through for the following week when I would be twelve weeks pregnant.

I was hesitant to tell Ursula and Roger about the birth center since they had always viewed pregnancy and birth as something very medical and complicated. I had always veered away from the medical side of birth and more into the idea that birth was the natural cycle of life. I didn't think of birth as being something that was dangerous, although I did understand how it could have that connotation for someone who had experienced the things the Stones had been through. The birthing center seemed like the perfect compromise, especially since I was eager to attempt a birth without resorting to an epidural, as I had for my two girls.

All my worrying was for naught when I finally did get up the nerve to ask the Stones about the birthing center. Ursula had a lot of questions, but in the end she told me that if it was what I wanted, it was something worth looking into.

We went to the birth center together the morning after I had a client deliver a little boy successfully. It was a few days before Christmas and I was happy and excited about my own pregnancy and birth, as well as the birth of a friend's child the night before. The spirit of the day was light and fun, and we all got along fabulously.

While Ursula and Roger looked over the financial papers, I had a great chat with the midwives' assistant and the receptionist about working in a birth center, and also about the role of a doula. I'd had a few friends offer their services and was really starting to get excited about the direction the journey was taking. We were facing challenges head-on, discovering favorable solutions for everyone involved. I can honestly say I was very happy with my decision to carry as a surrogate and was extremely pleased with the match that had resulted.

> In the end,
> it's not going to
> matter how many
> breaths you took,
> but how many
> moments took your
> breath away.
>
> —Shing Xiong

CHAPTER TWELVE
January 4, 2012

I ran my fingers through my hair, smiling at Ursula who sat across from me in the waiting room of the midwives' office. It felt awkward to be sitting in my doctor's clinic with Roger and Ursula. I had just met them, yet here I sat, carrying a baby for them and hoping that Roger would agree to stay in the waiting room when I gave birth to his child.

"You feeling okay today?" Ursula asked, placing her hand gently on my knee.

Her touch startled me a bit and I jerked back in my chair. "Um, fine. Yes. Thanks for asking."

"Crystal Kelley," the nurse called from the hallway to our left.

Ursula and I both stood, and from the corner of my eye I

noticed that her smile reflected mine, her teeth showing as her lips arched in an elated grin. As we walked out of the waiting room Roger and Ursula looked at each other. He nodded and she mouthed the words "I love you." It was cute to see them as a loving couple, excited to be creating another life, but it made me wish I also had someone by my side.

Roger said he wanted to stay out of the examining room. I remembered him telling me once that this was 'women's business' and that he would leave the doctor's visits to Ursula and me.

We were led to a room down the hall and to the right. I hopped up onto the examining table where the nurse took my temperature, pulse, and blood pressure. She then asked me to stand on the scale and I was surprised to see that I had gained a couple of pounds since my latest weigh-in. I had been sick a lot at the beginning of the pregnancy and had lost a few pounds, revealing my thin frame quite dramatically. At fourteen weeks I was finally gaining it back.

The nurse exited the room, leaving Ursula and me alone. We made small talk about how she and Roger planned to decorate the nursery and how our children were doing. A few minutes later Sarah, one of the midwives, opened the door. She wore a light pink nurse's uniform and as she entered she grabbed my right hand in both of hers, greeting me with a firm handshake. "You two ready to hear the baby's heartbeat?" she asked.

"We can't wait!" Ursula said.

Sarah squeezed the ultrasound gel onto my stomach and moved the fetal Doppler around in a circular motion. This was a very special moment, Stormie, when for the first time we heard the sound of your little life inside me—*thump, thump, thump.*

I grabbed Ursula's hand and she looked up at me with tears

in her eyes. I smiled back at her, excited that our partnership had worked and that you were thriving inside. With Ursula and Roger for parents, you were bound to have a good home, with access to great schools and everything you could ever need. I was glad to have found a couple so genuine and kind.

"So, Ms. Kelley, it says here that your due date is already determined to be June twenty-fifth. How did you get that date?"

"Well," I said, looking at Ursula for direction. Ursula had told me she wanted to initiate care with a provider before revealing the surrogacy but I was too nervous to disguise our relationship. "This was an IVF pregnancy."

"Ah, all right. Well that certainly does verify the conception date. So we'll go with the working due date and I guess that's about it. We're going to want to see you again in four weeks."

"Sounds good," I said.

Sarah and Ursula left the room while I got dressed. I could hear Roger's voice outside the examination room as the two women exited. He was having a discussion with the receptionist about the cost of services. I quickly finished dressing, almost falling down while I slid my feet into the legs of my jeans.

"Here she is," said the receptionist as I emerged into the hallway. "Ms. Kelley, the Stones can pay for your services but I need you to sign all the contracts, agreements, and medical releases. I'm not quite sure how you're planning to do this but your beneficiary doesn't have any influence on the signatures I need."

I felt myself beginning to turn red. For wanting to keep the surrogacy arrangement quiet they were doing a pretty good job of making it difficult.

"I'm sorry," I said, shuffling over to the nurses' station. "What do you need me to sign?"

■ ■ ■

I left the appointment consumed with the guilt of withholding information and I knew I wouldn't sleep unless I felt closure from the situation. Just as I was about to put my car into reverse, I pulled back into my parking spot and went back in to talk to the head midwife.

"I thought there was something a little unusual about the three of you," she said. "I'm glad you came to tell me. I think we're going to have a great working relationship. We've had other surrogates deliver here so we are aware of what needs to be done. Everything will be fine. Just know that we have no part in any of the legal work related to the matter, and the baby will have to leave in an authorized car seat with you in the same vehicle. We are here for you through your pregnancy and birth, Crystal. That is what you pay us for and that is what we do best. Just because they are paying the bill doesn't mean that affects the decisions and advice we give to you about your body."

"Thank you for understanding," I said, shaking her hand.

She gave me a hug and I turned to walk towards the front doors, my entire body glowing with relief.

JANUARY 18, 2012

I dreaded leaving the house for the cold December wind outside. Putting on our bulky winter coats, hats, and gloves meant it would take me an extra fifteen minutes just to get out the door with my children. I had another routine appointment scheduled to check on your progress, Stormie, and I needed to bring Emmy and Anne with me since we were going to a tree lighting in a

neighboring town afterwards and I didn't want to leave them with their grandparents. I had planned to meet Roger and Ursula at the doctor's clinic, and on the way they called to let me know they had something special they wanted to give the girls.

"Are they bringing us presents?" Anne asked from her car seat behind me.

"Presents? No. I don't think so, Sweetie."

Christmas was around the corner and it was the first year Anne understood the concept of Santa Claus and presents under the tree. I was working diligently to teach her about the kindness associated with Santa and the Christmas spirit. Our yearly Yule celebration was bustling from one holiday event to another, which made the girls particularly cranky at times. I hoped they would behave in the clinic.

■ ■ ■

"Hi, ladies," Roger said, standing to greet us in the waiting room. "Here's a little something for the two of you." He handed them a small container of butterscotch candies.

They took their gifts and ran over to a set of chairs positioned just below a large window, giggling while they unwrapped their candy, shoving one after another into their mouths.

■ ■ ■

"Are those people Santa's elves?" Anne asked as we got into the car afterwards.

"No, Honey. They're the people Mommy is carrying the baby for. Remember me telling you about them?"

"Hmm. Mmmm," she nodded, trying to buckle herself into her seat.

I heard a car door slam outside and looked over my shoulder at the black SUV parked behind me. A moment later the door opened and Roger emerged. He came over to my window and motioned for me to roll it down.

"Would you like to join us for lunch at the diner down the street? I saw they have a playscape."

"Yeah, that sounds like fun. We didn't really have any plans until later, so it's perfect," I replied.

He went back to his car and through my rearview mirror I saw Ursula smile. We drove the short distance to the small diner. It had a red and green plastic play set on top of Astroturf, enclosed in a fence along the back parking lot. We had already had enough snow to shut down Connecticut for weeks, and the cold chill as we walked past mounds of dirty gray snow sent shivers through me.

Once inside, we sat at a large booth towards the back of the restaurant.

"We're glad you could come with us," Ursula said, handing me a silver gift bag as we took our seats.

"Presents!" Anne exclaimed.

I instructed her to wait until we had ordered before opening the gift.

Almost immediately our waitress came over and took our order, her curly red hair pulled back in a festive snowflake headband. The second she turned to walk away, wrapping paper went flying, ribbons and packaging soaring into the air. Minutes later Anne and her sister ran to the playground holding their new

Barbie and Strawberry Shortcake dolls.

"You can play for a few minutes," I yelled to them, hoping not to disturb those sitting around us. "It's really cold out so I don't want you there for too long."

"How are you feeling, Crystal?" Ursula asked. "You look great."

"Oh, thanks. I feel okay. I'm not too sick or anything, so that's good. Just really tired."

"Yeah, I know," she said. "It's exhausting in the beginning."

I knew Ursula's response came from experience; something she knew she would never feel again. Even though, to me, it was hard to get out of bed some days, Ursula would probably welcome the lethargic mornings if it meant she could feel a baby growing inside her again.

"I just want to tell you how happy we are to have found you," Roger said. "We feel very blessed."

"I'm glad," I replied, lounging back in the chair to relax my aching lower back.

"Are you getting tired?" she asked, then turned to Roger. "We should go soon."

"I'm okay. It's really wonderful that you bought us lunch, and so thoughtful to bring presents for Emmy and Anne," I said. "You didn't have to do that."

"Well, it's almost Christmas," Roger said, "and we have a lot to be thankful for these days."

"You're giving us what we've always wanted," Ursula said, grabbing Roger's hand on the table. "The perfect baby."

"The perfect baby?" I asked, confused as to what she meant.

"We have a really good feeling this time," she said. "We never got to experience a normal pregnancy or a normal delivery, but this time it will be perfect."

I smiled and nodded at her. I didn't really understand what she meant by perfect. I've told you before, Stormie, that I believe all babies are perfect and I was already envisioning the ecstatic look on their faces when you were finally placed in their arms.

Our food was brought out and I motioned to Anne and Emmy to come in from outside.

"Have fun playing with your new dolls?" Roger asked, helping Emmy remove her jacket before sitting down.

"Yup," Anne said, already shoving the food into her mouth.

We finished our meal and Ursula and Roger stood up. Ursula reached out her arms ready to hug me.

"Thank you again for coming today," she said, squeezing me tightly. "I want you to know how special you are to us. You're giving us a wonderful gift. I hope you can come to think of us as family. After all, we're going to be connected for a very long time. You are going to be in our lives forever."

"Come on, dear. We should let Crystal rest," Roger said, grabbing Ursula's coat from the hook where it had been hung. "We'll call you tomorrow."

■ ■ ■

As I drove to the tree lighting I thought about her words. They were right: we did have a lot to be thankful for that season. The peace I found in my soul from Ursula's declaration made everything feel more brilliant. The tree lighting that night was magnificent and all the way home I rode the emotional high of feeling as if I was on top of the world.

The next morning, a fresh coat of snow covered the ground.

Since we lived in a small town up in the hills of New England, we had more snow than the main town. Plows did not come for almost two days but the simple living of the moment was beautiful. To me all was perfect.

This is how it's supposed to be, Stormie.

CHAPTER TWELVE

> Be faithful in small things because it is in them that your strength lies.
>
> —Mother Theresa

CHAPTER THIRTEEN
January 25, 2012

I had only seen Roger and Ursula a few times since we met in the park near my home. Today Ursula looked beautiful in a winter white coat that fell just above her knees, her hair pulled up into a smooth bun. She wore a blue and yellow scarf that peaked out of the top of her coat, perfectly positioned around her delicate neck.

We all met outside the doctor's practice and checked in with the receptionist together. I felt a little bit anxious as we took our seats in the waiting room—normal, I suppose, Stormie, given that we were finding out whether you were a boy or a girl. When my name was called, Ursula jumped up, while Roger stayed seated.

"You're not coming?" I asked Roger, looking down at him.

"Nah, this is a girl thing. I don't care one way or the other. 97
She's the one who wants a girl."

I glanced over at Ursula, who was beaming from ear to ear as she waited for me at the door to the examination rooms.

I shrugged. "Well, wish us luck, then," I said, turning to walk towards the exuberant Ursula.

We made our way into the tiny room, barely big enough for me to get past the bulky equipment. As I shuffled over to the examining table the technician gave me a few paper towels and told me to tuck them into my pants so I wouldn't get any of the gel on my clothes. We sat there awkwardly for a moment while he put all the information into the computer.

Ursula sat in a chair near the corner of the room. She was practically jumping. I could see the anticipation in her face as her eyes danced around the room and her smile grew bigger and bigger. In contrast, I was completely at ease. I was merely curious to see if there were any similarities with my other pregnancies, and if my gut feelings were correct.

"Are you nervous?" I asked Ursula.

"A little," she said sheepishly.

Silence filled the room a few moments before the technician looked over at us. She motioned for me to lie back, and pulled up my shirt to expose my bulging belly.

"My name is Andrea," she said, sitting down on a rolling chair in front of the monitor. "So let's see how your baby looks."

She put the cold gel on my stomach and moved the transducer around in a circular motion to get a good image of you. I wasn't a bit surprised, Stormie, that as usual, you were moving around quite a bit.

"You have a very active little one," she said.

CHAPTER THIRTEEN

"Yeah, tell me about it."

"Okay. So we're going to take a look and see how the baby's growing."

She worked quickly, looking at your different body parts and occasionally pointing something out on the screen while we watched.

"Can you tell whether it's a boy or a girl?" Ursula asked, leaning over me, straining to see the monitor.

"Are you hoping for one or the other?" Andrea asked.

I was quick to jump in. "I don't mind, but she really wants a girl," I said, pointing to Ursula, who looked over at me and smiled.

"She's right," Ursula said.

"Well, you're in luck, then!" Andrea exclaimed. She showed us the telltale trio of lines on the screen and printed off a picture for Ursula. "I'm almost done now," she went on. "I'm just having a hard time seeing the baby's heart clearly. This is why I really like to do ultrasounds at twenty weeks instead of early like this."

I was only eighteen weeks at the time, but since I lived an hour away from the birthing center they had arranged for me to have the ultrasound along with one of my routine scheduled visits.

"Do you think you'd be able to come back in a couple of weeks?" Andrea asked. "It won't cost anything extra."

Ursula's face softened as soon as she said it wouldn't cost any extra money. I knew they were having some difficulty with the financial aspect of the surrogacy because of my lack of medical insurance and the costly tests and medical fees they had incurred. With that concern alleviated, we agreed and another date was set for two weeks later.

■　■　■

Fourteen days had passed and I found myself in the same tiny ultrasound room, with the same technician, but without Ursula's anxiousness or Roger's stoic presence in the waiting room. They had been unable to get the time off work, so I was on my own for this visit. I was sure this would be a quick and easy appointment, so their absence did not bother me at all.

Sure enough, Andrea worked quickly and quietly. She was so fast with the transducer that I had a hard time keeping up. Being a doula, and having experienced several pregnancies myself and with friends, I was very familiar with the look of an ultrasound and had little trouble finding my way around a fetal picture. I made a few quick comments about certain body formations and talked about my previous pregnancies.

I was watching the ultrasound, more out of curiosity than anything, when an image flashed that I couldn't clearly interpret. And again, another. A dark line appeared to run from your nose to the top of your upper lip. I asked Andrea what it could be, wondering if you had a cleft palate, but she said she was going to let the doctor see for herself. She moved the transducer around a bit more and steadied it when she got to the heart. I tried to look but I knew this was out of my league. I had never been able to discern a baby's heart well in my own pregnancies, and I couldn't decide if what I was seeing was normal or not.

When she was done with the images, she printed a few and told me she would be right back. She gave me a copy of your profile image, and one of your feet. To me, Stormie, you looked perfect, your tiny little head and body so peaceful inside. I was so excited to see you at last. I glided the tip of my pointer finger across your picture and smiled, holding your image in my hands, wondering what you'd look like when you finally arrived. A few minutes later there was a knock on the door.

"Ms. Kelley?" The voice was unfamiliar. In walked another woman in a lab coat, older than Andrea, with short blonde hair cut in a bob. "How are you today?"

"I'm fine, thanks. What's going on?"

"Well..." her voice trailed off. "We're having some trouble with your baby's heart. I'm not sure if it's just the position she's in today or what, but we'd like to send you over to the hospital and get a more detailed ultrasound. Can we schedule you for something today?"

I told them I would have to get ahold of Roger and Ursula for the financial portion, but agreed to schedule another ultrasound date. *I can always cancel it*, I thought. And Stormie, you can guess that I was pretty keen to have another close look at you.

■　■　■

I left that appointment with another ultrasound scheduled. I hadn't told Roger or Ursula yet, as I knew they were both at work and wouldn't be able to answer the phone. It was a long drive home, and I just wanted to relax and listen to my music. I would call them later.

Suddenly, in the middle of one of my favorite songs, my cell phone began to ring. I scrambled to find my hands-free headphones while trying to concentrate on driving and answered it without even looking to see who it was.

"Hello?"

"Crystal, it's Ursula... this is terrible. We have to schedule another appointment. What could be the problem? Did you see anything on that ultrasound? I don't know what to do. We have to get..." The sound of Ursula's voice on the other end of the line was high pitched and frantic.

"Ursula... slow down!" I said, trying to listen to her and avoid traffic merging onto the highway at the same time. "What's the matter?"

"I got a call from the clinic. There's something wrong with the baby. Something about a cleft. But they wouldn't call for just a cleft. Something in the brain maybe? Oh, I don't know. I can't think straight right now. This is so horrible. We need to get you in for another ultrasound as soon as possible. Did you already leave? Can you go over there again today?"

She continued on, but at the same time my phone started to beep. I looked down and saw it was the midwife's office.

"Ursula, that's the midwives on the other end. Let me talk to them. Don't worry, we'll figure this out."

As I clicked over to the other line I took a deep breath. I knew the midwives would be able to tell me what was actually going on. Hopefully Ursula was blowing everything out of proportion. Either way I would get some answers by talking to them directly.

The woman on the phone said she was very concerned, more so for me than for Roger or Ursula, but it annoyed me that no one was showing any concern for you, Stormie. Anyway, as she explained, my initial reaction had been correct. It appeared that you had a cleft, which we agreed was no big deal. The other issues the tech had identified were that she was unable to locate your stomach, there was a potential problem with your heart, and something was appearing on the ultrasound in the cranial cavity that the doctor could not identify. It all seemed like very bad news for you, Stormie, but the midwife assured me that there were likely explanations for all the prospective problems you seemed to have, and that the doctors would be able to help us to sort out what was happening with you.

We talked about the hospital of choice and made the decision to try to get an appointment at a hospital that was a bit more local to me, since the one affiliated with the birth center was an hour's drive from my house. The appointment was scheduled in just three days. In the meantime, the midwives suggested I go to the lab and get the blood drawn for the quad screen that had been skipped the previous month. They stated that it would help to rule out some of the more common and typically fatal forms of birth defects.

Before she hung up, the midwife said something that stuck out to me. "Crystal, no matter what happens I want you to know that we are *your* doctors. We don't have any allegiance to the other doctors, the intended parents, or even to the baby. We are here as *your* medical advisors, and no one else's."

Her words made me nervous, Stormie, and at the same time they gave me a great sense of relief. Part of the initial worry we had all shared was that my pregnancy would be handled differently because of the surrogacy aspect. Her words validated my feelings and let me know that someone else would be there to legitimize my role in this process. I hoped you were as healthy as you appeared to me in your ultrasound pictures and that what had been revealed in your images were minor issues easily corrected.

When I got home, I took a nice long shower and made the girls dinner. Emmy was feeling especially needy that evening since I had been gone for most of the day. While she was almost two she still had many of the qualities I associate with toddlers. I didn't mind, though, and we spent an hour or so on the couch before bedtime, reading books and having tickle wars. My belly got in the way of a lot of our playing around, and at times Emmy would hit or bump me accidentally and you would get angry, kicking and punching me from inside in an attempt to get Emmy back. I was big enough that we could see the motions of your arms or legs as they pushed against my skin and made my belly roll like the waves of the ocean.

Emmy loved to follow your body parts, running her fingers over the area of skin that had just been pushed out until she found the protruding part. Sometimes she would laugh when that happened, and lay her hand over it as if she was trying to hold your hand or foot. I was quite sure you could feel this, Stormie, as it would almost immediately settle you, and we would go back to our books and games. It was amazing to me how the little life inside my belly and the little person who shared my space in the outside world could have such an interactive relationship. Sitting on the couch that night with Emmy's head resting on my belly, I took a video of your kicking and punching. You already seemed to have a little personality of your own. I sent the video to Ursula with the message, "She's so feisty already!"

As soon as I hit the send button I regretted doing so. I had almost forgotten about the appointment later in the week. I got Emmy ready for bed and hoped that my phone would stay silent for the rest of the night. It did, but I still slept very little.

■　■　■

The next morning at 7:15 a.m. my phone started to vibrate. I cringed, and turned over in bed. I was not ready to answer questions or talk about the appointment just yet. I wanted another hour of sleep, but after calling a couple of times Ursula began texting. Knowing I would never get back to sleep, I picked up my phone and read the three texts that were awaiting me.

'Crystal, how are you feeling after yesterday? I need the information for your next appointment so Roger and I can make sure to be there.'

'Crystal, please get the blood for the quad screen done today. They will need this at your appointment. Please also get the papers for the financial aid program.'

'Crystal, please let me know when your appointment is for the lab. They can call me and arrange for payment of the fee for blood work today.'

Fifteen minutes later, as I finished making coffee, the phone started ringing again. It was Ursula. I knew I would have to talk to her eventually, so I answered.

"Hi, Ursula. Did you get the video I sent you?"

"Hi, Crystal. Did you get my messages?"

"I did. I'll go to the lab this afternoon. I can email you the doctor's information. Ursula, doctors are wrong all the time. I'm sure whatever is up with the baby is something minor. A cleft lip isn't that big a deal. She's a strong baby. I make them that way."

"I know, I know. We'll take it one thing at a time. Be sure to get to the lab later, okay?"

"I will."

"Bye."

She hung up without saying anything further. Our conversation was very different from what I had become accustomed to. The pleasant phone calls of the past accompanied by questions about my family and light banter concerning the reality of being parents were completely absent. I was saddened by the

fact that she suddenly seemed so distant. At the same time I was
thankful for the shortness of the talk we had. Anne had woken
up and was systematically taking all her toys out of her room and
bringing them into the living room. I had a life to get to, and my
children were going to make sure it was busy.

Later that day I dropped the girls off with their grandfather
for a couple of hours while I went to the lab. It was a beautiful day
for February and I didn't even need to wear a jacket. I sat in my car,
relishing the heat that pummeled the windshield, and with my eyes
closed I let the energy permeate my body. In that moment I felt as
though nothing could go wrong.

I opened my door, locked the car, walked into the lab and
said hello to the receptionist. They had gotten used to seeing me
every few days as I had been in frequently during the weeks before
insemination, and were always excited to hear how things were
going. I didn't give them much information this time and asked for
the paperwork to get my blood drawn.

The lady I usually saw was out to lunch and her replacement
was not quite as gentle as I had come to expect. By the time I left the
clinic my arm hurt. As I walked to my car the phone rang again. It
was Ursula.

"Hey, Ursula. I'm just leaving the clinic now. They said it
would take about three days for the results to come in for the test.
Sorry, I couldn't get them to rush it."

"Hi, Crystal. Listen, we need to talk."

I stood next to my car, keys in hand ready to unlock the door.
"Sure," I said. "I'm sorry I haven't sent you the info for the doctor's
appointment yet. I've been pretty busy today."

"It's not about that. We've thought about it and I want you to
understand we don't think that this is your fault or anything."

"Of course not –"

"Hear me out," she interrupted. "We've thought about this a lot, and we consider ourselves to be pro-life, but we can't justify bringing a disabled child into the world."

Stormie, I felt like my heart stopped. I muttered something in reply, but she wasn't finished talking. She hinted, without actually saying it, that if anything was confirmed on ultrasound which they thought was too much to bear, she and Roger would ask for the pregnancy to be terminated.

My comments about taking it one step at a time, and reaffirming my personal pro-life stance were interrupted and talked over, and I started to stumble on my words. I'm not good under pressure, Stormie, and the sudden rush of adrenaline was starting to make you squirm, which made me even more anxious.

After a few minutes I knew I had to get off the phone. I was not prepared to have any more of that conversation with Ursula. I could not do this without falling apart. I had to stall for time. I tuned her out for a minute while I thought about what I should say.

"Ursula, all I can say is that we don't really have a whole lot of information right now. I told you from the start that I will not consider terminating unless the baby has some type of defect or deformity that would mean that she would die before she was born, or very shortly after. Now please, we should not even be talking about this until we have the appointment."

We hung up and you must have felt me shaking. You must also have heard my keys jingling uncontrollably in my hand as I tried to open the driver's side door. I got into my car and sat in the parking lot for a few minutes, then walked around the shops in the plaza. I was too shaken to drive and yet I wanted to get home where I could keep you safe.

I spent the next couple of days looking up everything I could about babies with clefts and a stomach that was unseen on an ultrasound. I wanted to be prepared and I had a ton of resources at my disposal. I asked some of the moms in my birth groups online if they had ever known anyone who had conditions such as esophageal atresia and clefts. I started collecting information about the surgery a child would need to treat the cleft and possible missing segment of the esophagus. Given the scant information, that was the most likely diagnosis I could find.

Ursula called a few times but I didn't feel up to having any more arguments, so I continued compiling my list of questions and information for the appointment.

On Thursday February 9, 2012 I arrived at the office of Maternal Fetal Medicine at Hartford Hospital. I was a few minutes early, so I sat in the waiting room and perused some of the magazines scattered on the table in front of me. I could feel my muscles tighten and my body temperature rise, as if an impending anxiety attack was about to erupt, but I managed to hold it together long enough to fill out the paperwork and await the sound of my name. Do you remember how I gently stroked you, Stormie, when I sensed you were also getting restless?

I secretly hoped that Roger and Ursula would miss the appointment. They had texted a couple of hours prior to let me know they were running late. Ursula asked me to have them wait, but in my anxious, nervous state I forgot to tell the nurse, and I walked into the examination room by myself.

The ultrasound technician who accompanied me was about eight months pregnant, and we chatted amicably about our babies.

When I asked her if it was difficult to work while pregnant she said, "It's okay. We see lots of babies, and I enjoy watching them in the womb." To this day I wonder if she regretted those words.

I was already bare belly on the examining table when Roger and Ursula arrived. They barged into the room very suddenly, not even giving me time to cover my exposed waistline. We had not spoken since that afternoon in the lab parking lot, and the moment they walked in my whole body tensed and my heart started pounding. They said hello and shook hands with the tech, and then Ursula gave me an awkward hug as she set her purse on the chair behind my head. I couldn't really see her, but the way her legs were pressed together and her hands clasped in her lap, I knew she was nervous.

"All right, we're going to start again," the technician said. But before she could even begin, Ursula piped up.

"Will we be able to find out exactly what's going on with the baby today?"

The tech looked up at her, surprised. "We'll take a look and see what we can see, but ultrasounds are not perfect. I'm going to do an initial scan and see what areas we need the doctor to look at."

She started scanning my belly, speaking out loud as she identified body parts and internal organs. She never said anything specific, just occasionally things like, "and this is not what we normally see here" when she came to what had been identified as a possible defect. Behind me I could hear Ursula sniffling, accompanied by the occasional squeak of the chair as she moved and dragged it along the floor.

"I'm going to need to get the doctor now," the technician said, standing up and turning the monitor off.

As she left the room Ursula started to talk. She didn't get much out before the doctor and technician arrived in the room. Dr. Mansfield was a tiny lady, swimming in a white coat and carrying a notebook and pen. She quickly stepped over to the ultrasound monitor and turned it on. She worked quickly, looking at the pictures the tech had taken, asking technical questions. We all listened intently, trying to make some sense of what they were saying.

Finally she spoke to us. "It seems we have something to discuss," she said. "Your baby has some abnormalities."

"Abnormalities?" Ursula asked.

"Yes. I don't know the extent of them yet but..." the doctor pointed to the monitor. "See the head here?"

"Hmm. Mmm," I replied in unison with Ursula.

"Your baby has a cleft lip."

I leaned in to look at your picture more clearly and could see what the doctor was pointing to. Your lip looked separated, as if the top of your jaw line was split in two.

They can deal with a cleft lip, I thought, wishing at that moment that I could rest my hand reassuringly on your restless little limbs.

"A cleft lip is easily corrected. Right?" Ursula asked.

"It can be, but unfortunately there's more," the doctor said. "I can't seem to find the stomach and there may be some heart problems to deal with."

Dr. Mansfield handed her a tissue, apologizing as he reached across me.

"How could the baby not have a stomach?" Roger said. "That's impossible."

"Are you thinking she could have esophageal atresia?" I

CHAPTER THIRTEEN

interrupted.

The doctor blinked at me. I don't think she expected me to have any idea about the condition. "It's a possibility."

"That requires one surgery, right? Immediately after birth? Then she'd be fine."

"Well, that's right," the doctor said. "But when we see one defect and then two defects, we start looking for more defects. When there are a number of things that go wrong, then we start looking for some underlying cause of the defects. And her heart seems very complicated. I can't even tell you what would happen with her heart as I'm not a cardiologist. All I can tell you is that she would probably need multiple operations to repair it, if it is even operable."

"But it's still fixable?" I asked. Tears were welling up in my eyes. To me, this doctor was hammering nails in the coffin for you long before it was warranted. She talked about you as if your life meant nothing; like you weren't even a person at all. You were just the broken 'fetus.' Not the strong feisty little person I had come to know.

Roger had some questions as well. They were good ones, things I would never have thought of. Ursula's questions were more motherly. Would you be able to play with the other children? Would you be able to walk? The one thing they both kept referring to was the notion of normalcy. Would you be normal?

This infuriated me. What was normal? Who were they to decree what was normal and what wasn't.

Dr. Mansfield's answer to that was fairly simple. "No heart baby is a *normal* baby."

I said nothing, Stormie, as I would have exploded if I had. Instead my emotions had ignited a fire in my chest and I held back from the growing urge to stand up and leave.

"Where do we go from here?" Roger asked.

"Well, I'd like to do a fetal echo," the doctor said. "And we could do an amniocentesis to confirm the ultrasound findings but that has its risks too. If you have time today we can get that done right away."

From behind me a quiet voice cut the silence. So quiet, Stormie, that I'm sure it wasn't meant to be heard.

But I heard every damning word—

"But what would be the point?"

> Sometimes you
> have to stand
> alone just to make
> sure you still can.
>
> —Unknown

CHAPTER FOURTEEN
March, 2002

I **sat alone on the steps of a church basement.** It was early March, and the foreboding St. Louis air sent a cruel reminder of just how unforgiving the winter had been.

I was nineteen, nearly twenty and I had nowhere to go. The woman I worked for went on a rampage, throwing all my bedding out on the front yard and locking the door to the only home I had known. I expected no less since I had reported her to child protective services previously because she used cocaine. Her family lived in five houses on that street, so I didn't dare go back. I had seen what happened to people who had disagreements with her family and I did not want to end up in the hospital, or the morgue.

But I still had nowhere to go. My dad was away taking care

of my dying grandfather so I couldn't call him. My mom was... well, we weren't exactly on speaking terms after I had taken the job. At the time, my only concern was a roof over my head and a place to cook food so I could eat. I didn't know I was moving in with a drug addict. And the kids were so sweet. How could I leave them? My mother wouldn't understand, and she would probably tell me—'I told you so.'

I scrolled through the faces of friends and family in my mind but couldn't think of anyone to rescue me, so I curled up and leaned against the wall of the enclave in the church, thankful for the barrier from the wind. However, it would have been nice to cozy up with a blanket and a warm fire. The cold and I didn't get along, and I found it hard to see any bright side to my current situation.

A middle aged couple walked by. "Should we help her?" whispered the woman to the older gentleman holding her hand.

The man chided her, "Oh come on, not another one of your druggie charity cases. Just leave her be," and rushed her along.

I shook my head at the irony.

FEBRUARY 9, 2012

I sat in the bathroom with my head in my hands. Thanks to my once again rising anxiety, you had woken up and moved a bit, kicking your legs and your arms.

I stroked my belly gently, hoping to soothe you. "Are you really that bad off, Stormie?" You did not respond, and yet I was sure you were listening.

"So what do I do?" Silence.

"I guess I'm on my own, huh?" You nudged me as if to make sure I knew you were still there. I laughed. At least you seemed to have good comedic timing.

I stood up and readjusted myself. My eyes were red, yet I had barely even noticed I was crying. I stared at my image in the mirror, mascara running down my face, and asked myself what I had gotten into. I would have done anything to keep from going back into the room. There in the bathroom I could pretend nothing was wrong, hiding behind the broken girl in the mirror. The second I walked out the door I would have to deal with reality again. It was not something I looked forward to.

A few moments froze in time—my moments to breathe and gather the strength to tell them how I really felt. I inhaled and exhaled slowly, then walked out of the bathroom.

As I approached the room I could hear Ursula and Roger talking to the doctor. I stopped briefly outside the door and listened to their mumbling voices on the other side of the wall. Dr. Mansfield was explaining the amniocentesis test and giving them information about its accuracy, risks, and flaws. Ursula asked about something else, something I couldn't make out, and Dr. Mansfield told her, "Well it's really up to Crystal. Crystal is the patient."

"Yes, how about we talk to the patient?" I said, storming back into the room. "Let's not forget who the patient is."

Ursula's face turned a light shade of pink, displaying her embarrassment for whatever question she had asked. In that moment, I was thankful I hadn't heard it.

"So, are we ready for the amnio?" Dr. Mansfield said.

"Sure. As long as they say it's okay." My voice trembled as I glanced over at Ursula and Roger.

The doctor looked at them, then Roger stood up. "We have some questions of our own and we'd like to discuss them in private."

"Of course," the doctor said. "Crystal, I'm going to escort

Mr. and Mrs. Stone to an office down the hall, and we'll get you all prepped and ready."

■　■　■

Being prepped for an amniocentesis is probably one of the scariest things I have ever done while pregnant. As a more naturally-minded person, I have always thought that if the need arose for an amnio, I would most likely decline it. But I really wanted to be able to put the minds of the Stones at ease, and this seemed like the most logical way to do so. The room bustled around me as several nurses came in. One had me undress my top half and put on a gown, while another brought in a package with instruments wrapped in blue sterile fabric, followed by someone else carrying paperwork for me to fill out. As I grabbed the pen and papers she handed me, I realized that once again, I was shaking.

I took a deep breath, Stormie, fixed my mind on you and willed my body to cooperate. The nauseous feeling that had become normal in early pregnancy but had subsided weeks ago came rushing back as you flip-flopped in my belly. I closed my eyes and told the nurse who was perched at the end of the examining table that I needed a moment alone. She quickly stood up and ushered everyone out of the room. With the prying stares gone, I sat up, crossed my legs on the table, and pulled up my shirt.

"Listen here, little girl," I said, talking directly to the rippling skin that told me exactly where you were, "this is not going to work if you keep flopping around in there. I know you're sensing my fear, and I'm not going to lie and say that I'm not afraid 'cuz there would be no point. But I would never forgive myself if they hurt you with the amnio needle, or if the test caused me to lose you, so please,

Stormie, just settle down for mama."

I took a few deep breaths to calm my own nerves and was about to get up and let the nurses back in the room when there was a knock on the door.

"Come in," I called.

Dr. Mansfield walked into the room. Her stern expression, her clenched jaw and her eyes slightly squinted immediately caused me to panic. Beads of sweat formed on her brow as she closed the door behind her and walked towards me. She looked at me, and then down at her hands as she sat on the end of the bed.

"Crystal, they don't want to go forward with the amnio."

"What?" I cried out. "What do you mean? Why not?"

"They don't believe that the results of the amniocentesis will make a difference. We wouldn't have the full results back for at least a few more weeks, and that takes us out of the timeframe during which it is possible to terminate the pregnancy and therefore they do not wish to have you undergo the testing."

"*Termination?* Who said anything about termination? We don't even know what's wrong with the baby. That was the point of coming here; to find out what's wrong. We still don't even have any answers!"

It was quite uncanny, Stormie. As if you understood the severity of the situation, you moved forcefully inside me, lurching my belly from one side to the other.

Dr. Mansfield sighed and put her hands on mine. "They feel as though it is all just too much. They would like to talk to you."

My head spun as I tried to piece together what she was saying. A nurse came in to help me wipe the ultrasound gel off of my belly and would hardly even look at me, her eyes staring down at the floor the entire time.

SAVING STORMIE: THE BABY S STORY

After all the gel was cleaned off me, Dr. Mansfield and the nurse exited the room, leaving me to ponder what had just happened.

"It's okay," Stormie," I said, placing my hands on my belly to comfort you. "I won't let anything happen to you."

I was confused and bewildered as I got my shirt back on and gathered up my purse and book. Dr. Mansfield waited outside the room to escort me down the winding hallway and through several doors before we reached the office where the Stones were waiting. The sign on the door read 'Genetic Counselor.'

JULY 15, 2003

The sun was hot, too hot for me, but I was still there. I shaded my eyes to see if I could find the person I was looking for across the track. Standing on my tip-toes I peered over the heads of the other spectators. Suddenly there was a tap on my back, "Looking for me?"

I spun around, surprised to see my friend behind me. How had he managed to get through the crowd of people? His wheelchair wasn't the smallest piece of equipment, and the track was busy that day.

"What are you doing over here?" I asked. "I thought you were racing today."

"I am," Ryan responded. "My race isn't until later. Want to get something to eat?"

As we made our way out of the crowded spectator area, I spotted several of the kids I had been working with during practice the previous week, huddled together under one of the tents. We joined them for a few minutes before heading over to the food area. One of the girls, Jamie, looked hot and flustered, her hair matted to her face as she fanned herself with a stack of flyers. Jamie's mother stood behind her, trying to get her to take the water bottle and drink a little.

"Mo-om," she whined, "leave me alone. I'm fine. I'll get my own water!"

The kids were engrossed in the event. This was a big track meet and many of their friends from other states would soon be arriving to participate in the day.

I had known these kids for most of their lives and knew many of their stories. Jackie had spina bifida, exactly like my childhood best friend, Amanda. I had not seen Amanda for many years, but that had nothing to do with her disability; we had simply grown apart. Spending years as best friends, though, I had become involved with the Cruisers, a wheelchair sports club that was operated out of one of the local hospitals. I met Jackie at her first practice when she was only a few years old. She was bright and always had a smile on her face. She used a wheelchair when I first met her, but at about ten years old she graduated to walking with the help of braces and crutches. She had such a bubbly personality and was one of the most talkative kids I knew. At fourteen she was a force to be reckoned with on the track and also one of the biggest pranksters in the group.

I saw Adam sitting on the sidelines, slightly set apart from the others. He'd had a brain tumor which caused him to lose the use of his legs. But in a race-chair he was one of the fastest nine-year-olds in the country. He was a quiet kid, and it took a little bit of effort to get him to open up, but once he did he could tell you anything and everything you wanted to know about the science behind racing, wind resistance, and the best ways to get a tactical advantage.

Then there was Addah. She was only five, and had developmental delays, but her personality set her apart from everyone else. The older kids would gather around her to hear her jokes. However, when it was time to be serious, nobody could break her focus. She was already showing her determination in practices. As defense for her team she did not always stop her opponent, but she consistently gave it her best effort.

We passed several families I did not know as we made our way over to the food area. Each one had a happy, smiling child, and parents who were racing around getting everything ready. Some of the kids had breathing tubes, others were tube fed. Some were in wheelchairs, and others used crutches or a walker. The important thing about them all, though, was that they were there together. The event at the race track was about trying to be the best you could be. For those kids, it may not have been a five minute mile. It may have meant a few extra breaks between shot-put throws, or using adaptive equipment such as the specialized racing chairs that many athletes were cruising around in. But for me, the most important part of the day was the realization that these children, though different, were really not all that disparate.

This was a lesson I had learned a long time ago. Growing up with a best friend with a disability meant taking a lot of flack from other people. I was the one standing up for my friend when others tried to bring her down. I knew what those nasty words did to her feelings about herself, and I knew how much it meant to her to have someone who would tell those who spoke nasty words to shut their mouths. As time went on, I found that the special-needs kids in my school seemed drawn to me. I became the person who would stand up for them, defend them against those who spoke ill of them. I also saw each one of them grow; they blossomed into individuals who were able to express themselves and tell others how their words and actions affected them. Through that experience I started my path of volunteering with the adaptive sports team, and the experiences there showed me how much joy and how much meaning a person's life can have, even if they are disabled. It's a lesson I never forgot, even after my best friend and I stopped talking to each other. When my younger sister was diagnosed with epilepsy I became more of a caregiver than just her sister. I taught her how to read, and we spent countless hours together doing projects and activities to keep her learning and developing while my mother rested from the daily burden of her physical care.

"Hey! Earth to Crystal."

Ryan had returned with our food. I didn't even realize that I had been sitting in the sun, daydreaming.

"You're sweating like crazy. Come sit in the shade," he said.

He moved his legs so that I could sit on the end of his chair. This wasn't anything uncommon, but I was still aware of the looks I got from some of the passing spectators and athletes. He saw them too, and smiled at me.

"Let them look," he said as he pulled me over for a kiss. I started blushing and stood up quickly, causing him to lose his balance and topple over. We both started laughing, and he turned the chair right-side up. "Come on down here. Let's eat."

FEBRUARY 9, 2012

As the door to the genetic counselor's office opened I caught a glimpse of someone seated behind a large oak desk. She was a curvy woman, with curly hair and glasses, her hands folded on top of a pile of paperwork.

"Hello, everyone," she said. "I'm here to help you understand the complications your baby has developed and the options you have in front of you. I'm a geneticist and I specialize in the kind of issues your baby has. You'll have to make some very hard decisions and I can tell you that this process is not an easy road to take." She paused and looked directly at me. "Crystal, the Stones have decided that they do not wish to pursue an amnio at this time. They do not feel that it would be relevant to the decision that needs to be made, as the results will take a long time to come back and they have made a decision already."

"We don't intend to bring another child with disabilities into this world," Ursula said.

"So you want to abort?" asked the geneticist, her eyes darting back and forth from the Stones to me, as if she was trying to read what was going on in our minds.

The walls closed in on me, Stormie. I could feel my heart race, and blood rushed to my head, making me feel as though I would pass out at any moment. I started to see spots, and the talking in the room became a garbled conversation I could no longer hear properly or understand.

"We don't see any other option. We can't go through with having another disabled child," Roger said. "We've discussed it and we'd like to terminate the pregnancy."

> Do not count
> the days;
> make the
> days count.
>
> —Muhammad Ali

CHAPTER FIFTEEN
February 9, 2012

I sat staring at Roger and Ursula in utter disgust. I clenched my jaw tightly and grabbed the edge of my chair, gripping it as hard as I could in an effort to release my anger rather than lunging at either of them.

"How can you say that?" I asked, their blank stares stirring up more rage inside me.

"What do you mean?" the geneticist asked, her gaze continuously shifting between Roger and Ursula and me, waiting for one of us to answer.

I glared back at her. "We don't even know what's really wrong with her. You doctors are wrong all the time. You misdiagnose babies with horrible things and they come out fine.

How can you give up after one test says she has a cleft, maybe a heart problem, and something strange going on with her stomach? I mean, really. Babies don't develop without a stomach, so obviously there's more we need to explore there. But to say she's never going to have a chance at a normal life—how the hell do you define normal?"

I realized I was shouting and sat back in my chair with my head in my hands. I could feel the weight of you in my belly as silent tears began to form. I thought about your little life and how peaceful you were in your current state.

"We've thought about this a lot, Crystal." Roger's voice commanded attention but he spoke to me softly as he explained their decision. "I have medical training. I know what it entails for children like this. Our daughter was born with a heart defect. To think that I could have spared her suffering makes me want to do for this child what I could not do for her."

"We couldn't free our daughter from the pain; we didn't know. But this time we can." Ursula was practically whispering, but her words cut through the air loud and clear.

"I'm sorry, Ursula, I can't do it. I told you this the other day. I may be pro-choice when it comes to other people, but when it comes to me, I'm pro-life."

"Please," she said, "you know we are Catholics. We are pro-life just as much as you are. But we have to think about what God's will would be for this baby. I can't believe that God would want a child to be born to endure so much suffering. Maybe if she just had a cleft it would be different, but all this together is too much. He would want us to end her suffering. Please, think about that. We need you to be God-like, we need you to make that decision and not let our baby suffer."

My mouth dropped open and for a moment I stopped listening, fading off into my own thoughts. Had she really said that? Did the words 'be God-like' just come out of her mouth in reference to ending the life of a child?

Now, I am not a Catholic, Stormie, nor am I a Christian. I have my own belief system that I feel very strongly about. But I also attended a Catholic high school, and I am very aware of the Church's stance on abortion as well as their beliefs about the will of God. The words that Ursula spoke to me sounded nothing like what I had been taught during my four years in Catholic school. They were nothing like what I had heard for years growing up in a Protestant family, attending church every Sunday.

Still bewildered, I looked up, glaring into Roger's eyes. "This is not about God," I said. "This is about you. This is about you wanting to play God. God would want nothing to do with this."

I faded out again, traveling somewhere warmer and bright, where the darkness could not reach me. But soon that sunlight became grim. Dark, treacherous clouds closed in, threatening to pull me back to my harsh new reality. I wished for it all to go away but it would not.

"Why are you doing this to us?" Ursula asked.

After a few moments of silence the near-whisper of Mrs. Stone brought me back to awareness. Everyone stared at me, awaiting an answer. I have never been good under pressure, and the only thing running through my head was, *Why me? Why me? Why my baby?*

Shaken, I replied, "I'm not doing anything *to* you. *You* wanted this baby."

My heart started pounding and I realized that if I stayed in that office any longer I might explode with rage. Much like when I used to fight with my mother as a teenager, I blurted out what had been going through my head from the moment I heard the word 'termination.'

"You gave this baby to me to protect and that's exactly what I'm going to do."

Before they could utter another stammered word, I walked out the door. The geneticist sprang from her desk and hurried out after me. I had no idea where I was going. The hallways were a maze and I couldn't remember from where I had come. All I knew was that I needed to get away from everyone in that room.

"Please, Crystal, come in here," the geneticist called from a short distance behind me. She was holding a door open, and as I stood there trying desperately to make some sense of where I was going, she smiled at me. "I'm not on anybody's side," she said.

I followed her into what looked like a conference room. There was a long table in the middle of the room, with two dozen or more chairs around it. Another door at the other end of the room led out towards the reception area. She stepped past me and closed that door, so that we were alone and undisturbed.

"I can sit with you if you need someone to talk to," she said.

I did not reply. I sat in the chair closest to the exit and placed my purse on the floor next to me. The geneticist pulled up another chair and sat close to me.

"You okay?" she asked.

I nodded, but the tears had already started to flow. "No. Not really." I stared down at the white tiled floor. "I can't do this. I can't do this. How can they even ask me to do this? They know how I feel. I've never *not* told them how I feel."

I took a deep breath. I had seen this coming and had dreaded this appointment. I had even waited until the last possible moment to tell them the time so that I might have a remote possibility of finding out the news alone. After the discussion Ursula and I had a couple of days earlier, I suppressed a lingering feeling that their minds were already made up. As I cried, my thoughts became words. I told the geneticist everything I felt and even revealed my own personal experiences. I talked about my children and asked her how I should explain to them that I was not going to have a baby anymore. Every racing thought that went through my head passed over my lips and into the ears of the woman sitting next to me. When I finished talking, we sat in silence for a few minutes before she stood up.

I sat glaring at the door, hoping for an escape. I was surprised when she came to my chair and put her arms around me. I began to sob into her satin blouse. I'm sure I ruined it but I couldn't stop. When I finally caught my breath, she grabbed my shoulders, pulling me away from her as she looked into my eyes.

"This isn't easy for anyone. I'm sure Mr. and Mrs. Stone truly feel they are doing the best thing for this baby, just as you do. A decision, however, does need to be made, but it does not need to happen right now. And just so you know, I think it was really poignant what you said back there about them playing God. I think they will have a lot to think about when they leave here today."

"Do I have to go back in there?"

"No. I'll show you out. If you would like to schedule another appointment, I'd be happy to do that for you. We'll want to see you in two weeks, and depending on how things have worked out here we'll probably do the fetal echo then."

I felt a knot in my throat as I walked up to the receptionist's desk. I had no idea how long it would take for the Stones to realize I had left. I wanted to leave before they came looking for me.

I was so preoccupied that I didn't even notice that the pregnant technician who had done the scan was standing behind the desk. As I took my appointment card and turned to leave, she grabbed my hand.

"You're not going to terminate?" she asked, motioning to the card in my hand.

"I don't want to. I don't really know what I'm going to do, though. I don't know that I have much choice." The tears started to well up again.

"I'm sorry, I didn't mean to upset you. I'm sure this has all been really difficult. I see parents come through here every day. They find out something is wrong with their baby and then we never see them again." She put her hand on her own swollen belly. "I always wonder what happened to those babies—if their parents chose to keep them or if we caused their lives to end. It's a horrible feeling sometimes, knowing that people come in here and hang on every word the doctors say, never giving those babies a chance."

She seemed anxious, as though she was not supposed to be talking to me.

As I thanked her, she slipped a second appointment card into my hand. "If you need anything," she whispered, and hurried away.

I walked out of the office, nervous in case I saw the Stones on my way out. I did not want to talk to them, and I certainly didn't want them to make any attempt at initiating more conversation. Pacing up and down past the elevators, I finally looked at what the technician had given me. She had written her personal phone number on the card along with her name, Sarah. I slipped it in my pocket as I entered the elevator, thankful that I

CHAPTER FIFTEEN

had someone on my side.

When I finally made it to the parking garage and into my car, I took the card out of my pocket and looked at it. Her name was written in small letters, all capitals. The number underneath had been traced over several times, as if she had written it before I even came to the checkout desk. When I turned the card over I realized that she had also written her email address on the back. I set it aside, uncertain if I would call her or not, and picked up my phone. There was one very important phone call I had to make.

"Mom? It's me."

> All things are
> difficult before
> they are easy.
>
> —Thomas Fuller

CHAPTER SIXTEEN
May, 1999

I **remember it as though it was yesterday.** The steps of my high school were getting a bit too familiar as I waited for my mother to pick me up, their cold, rough exterior grainy under the palms of my hands. I stared out at the circular drive in front of me, stretching my neck to see each car as it passed on the road ahead, hoping one of them would be her. I waited for almost an hour, then decided to walk down to my friend's house. Sharlene was used to me showing up on her doorstep a few times a week. I lived too far to walk, so if I did not have a ride by the time they locked the school doors, I was on my own. Sometimes I would sit there until it started to get dark, all expectation for my mother's arrival diminishing by the minute as it grew colder. Walking would keep me warm, and

Sharlene's mother was always home, ready to serve hot chocolate and after-school snacks.

I picked up my backpack and began the fifteen minute walk. I wished I had agreed to go over to her house earlier when she asked me at the lockers, but at that time I thought my mom was picking me up sooner than she usually did—if she remembered.

As I walked I couldn't help thinking that I was going to look like an idiot showing up just before dinner. Suddenly my pocket started buzzing; my pager was going off. I jogged the last block to Sharlene's house and her mother met me at the door.

"Can I use the phone?" I asked, breathless. As I called the number back, I inhaled deeply, both to calm my nerves and to make it sound like I had not just been running.

"I'm at the school. Where are you?" Her voice came through the speaker like a sharp tack, piercing my ear drums.

"I walked to Sharlene's. Guess I'll see you in a minute."

I shook my head, disappointed that once again she blamed her absence on me. She would make sure I would hear about it on the way home.

FEBRUARY 9, 2012

My conversations with my mother had been brief until this point. Ever since the long talk we had before I decided to pursue surrogacy, we had kept in contact, but only barely. She would call every so often to check on me and the kids, and we texted back and forth a few times a week. She made it clear that she was there for me, but with her own set of rules and boundaries. When I was finally on my own she offered advice and help when I needed it, but always on her own terms. Often I felt demeaned by our interactions, so I had not told her about the ultrasounds. I didn't want to appear immature, or desperate, if it truly turned out to be nothing. Our relationship had become good over the years when we spent our time apart, but she still looked at me as a little girl and I wanted her to see me as an adult.

Today all that was irrelevant. Just as when I was young and felt really down, or had a big problem to solve, my mom was the one I ran to. I felt like the child she saw me as, unsure of what I was supposed to do or where I could go to find the answer. I was overwhelmed with conflicting thoughts, confused by the words of the doctors, teetering between tears and clenched fists.

I needed some guidance—someone with a clear head and an analytical mind to talk through the situation with me. I knew no one better to call than my mother. Even when I had wanted her to do things for me so that I could take the easy way out, she had always pushed me to work things out, guiding me towards the right steps to make adult decisions. I knew she would have a good insight on the situation and I really needed someone to tell me something that made sense.

I had received her voicemail and returned her phone call, only to leave a message on her phone. "I really need to talk to you. Something's wrong with the baby and I don't know what to do."

I made the drive home, a million things racing through my head. Yet, if anyone had asked me what I was thinking, I am not sure I could have identified a single thought.

When I pulled into my driveway I stayed seated in the car. Twenty minutes passed before I realized that I had forgotten to stop at my in-laws' house to pick up the girls. As I headed back towards town the reality that this was not going to go away started to set in.

CHAPTER SIXTEEN

■ ■ ■

I avoided eye contact with Scott's parents, unable to make any normal conversation. Several times I could see his mom's lips begin to form a word, but she held back her questions and didn't push the subject. For that I was grateful. I had no idea what to say. How do you tell someone that you've just been told you have to get an abortion?

I put the girls in the car and drove back home. It was dark by the time we pulled into the driveway, and both Anne and Emmy were asleep in the back. I closed my eyes, taking in the silence. I tried to forget the events of the day, but a timely little nudge in my belly from you, Stormie, quickly brought it all back. I peered in the rearview mirror at the girls. What would I have done if I had found out they had some devastating illness or deformity when I was pregnant with them? Would it make my love for them any less powerful? Would I have tried to run away from the issue, giving up on my babies? It had been awful enough placing Anne into the arms of a stranger when she had her heart surgery, but would I have ever chosen not to give her life because of that difficulty?

My phone rang. It was my mom. I snapped back to attention, and almost immediately tears started to well up in my eyes again. I was already crying by the time I answered.

"Crystal, I only have a few minutes but you sounded really upset. What happened?"

"There's something wrong with her mom. The doctors say that she has a heart problem and something about not seeing her stomach?"

"Crystal. Babies don't develop without a stomach. What did they say they thought was wrong with her stomach?"

"I don't even know. They said they didn't see one. It didn't matter because I was going to do the amniocentesis and then the intended parents decided they didn't want it done. They want to end the pregnancy."

"What do you mean? You were going to do an amnio? What the heck happened? I know you, you wouldn't do an amnio."

"She has a cleft. She has a heart problem. She has something wrong with her brain but they have no idea what it is. They can't see her stomach. They said it was probably all related and that the next thing we should do is an amnio. So I said okay. But Roger and Ursula said no to the amnio and they want to get rid of her instead. I don't." I started to cry again. "I don't know if I can go through with it."

"Damn it, Crystal. I don't have time to talk about this right now. Can I call you tomorrow?"

"I guess so," I said, feeling defeated and abandoned, just as I had on the school steps all those years ago.

"In the meantime, what does your contract say? You know what... oh, never mind. Send me a copy of your contract. I can't imagine you signed anything that said you would terminate. Did you? Did you read what you signed?"

"Of course I did, Mom. I even had them change it but it was still really vague."

"Crap. I have to go. Email it to me, and don't do anything until I've called you back, okay?"

"Yeah. Okay."

While driving home I had daydreamed about all the things she would say and what I would say back. To be cut off that quickly left me with nothing more than confusion and a sense of emptiness I couldn't shake off.

I got out of my car and brought in my sleeping daughters one by one. Emmy woke up as soon as I unbuckled her seatbelt, and asked to sleep on the couch with me. I gathered her pillow and blanket in my arms, but she wanted to lay her head on my lap while I sat on the couch.

I grabbed my laptop and logged in, trying to escape my thoughts. I had an email in the account I had set up for communication with the surrogacy agency. It was from my agent, Sharon.

> Dear Crystal,
>
> I heard there have been some complications and would like to meet with you.
>
> Please call me and let me know when will suit you. I will come to you.
>
> Sharon

I closed Sharon's message and saw another email below it, from a surrogacy lawyer I had contacted before the ultrasound.

> Dear Crystal,
>
> Let me know what the doctor says. Then we can speak. You have a constitutional right to decline to terminate but probably the intended parents can then stop paying you.
>
> We can discuss further after you know more.
>
> One good option would be to go to a counseling session with the intended parents and try to resolve this with the help of a trained professional.
>
> Veronica Ferris

It was good to know that there was no way they could force me to terminate, but that did not solve any of my problems.

I opened up my browser, writing to everyone from the forums who I thought might have an idea of what I should do. I also contacted several women from my due date groups on Facebook, desperate for anyone to reply with advice. I knew I would be able to get a number of different opinions from the ladies in my groups.

I immediately received responses. Some thought as I did and others were adamantly opposed.

Sometime close to midnight I finally shut down the computer and carried Emmy into my room. Snuggling up with her and feeling you settle into a comfortable position, Stormie, made everything feel okay again. Even though I knew I would have to face another day, I decided to leave my demons for the morning.

■　■　■

'That baby is not yours. It's not your choice,' one blogger said.

'Shame on you, Crystal. This isn't your decision to make,' said another.

They went on and on, proclaiming to everyone that I should be shunned from their tight-knit groups. I was the reason surrogacy got a bad rap, some said. I should never have been allowed to be a surrogate, said many more posts.

I sat and sat, crying at the pages and pages of nasty comments defaming my reason for becoming a surrogate. With a few short words, these strangers had managed to turn me into a dreadful human being, hated by women across the world. Were they right? Was I really being selfish? After all, Stormie, one of the reasons I had chosen gestational surrogacy was because you would not be genetically related to me. These two people who were asking me to abort were, as I believed, the biological sources of the genes that made up your DNA. What was going to happen if they did not take responsibility for you?

I was so torn, Stormie. I did not intend to raise another child. I needed to devote my time to caring for the two I already had. I wanted to enjoy the pregnancy without the inherent stress of preparing for and caring for a newborn, but this didn't stop me caring passionately for you while I carried you, and wanting nothing but the best for you. And while I did not see the defects diagnosed by the doctor as fatal, I did understand the complexities that congenital heart defects can involve. My own daughter was born with a defect. We were very lucky that she only required one surgery, but I know many people with children who had to see the cardiologist regularly and who have had multiple operations. They have an added element of their life that others can never understand, yet these people live happy, productive, and meaningful lives.

Thankfully, my friends and acquaintances around the United States chimed in on my own webpage in support of me, their comments proclaiming outrage that someone would ask to terminate a child they had purposely created. Some questioned the diagnosis, others praised God and quoted pro-life propaganda. One lone comment declared that I should keep my private problems off Facebook. It became a war of words on my page between those who supported me and those who felt I was completely in the wrong. I quickly deleted some of the posts and sent many of my friends a message inviting them to join me in my private group to talk. The group buzzed with disapproval for Roger and Ursula, some directing me to call a lawyer, or to get a second opinion. Others even suggested I sue. It became overwhelming.

Suddenly at the bottom of the screen a private message popped up. A good friend of mine sent me a link.

'Crystal, is this you?'

When I clicked on the link, it led me to a story that sounded very familiar. A mother of two; a baby with a cleft and heart defects; the parents wanted the surrogate to abort. I commented at the bottom of the article, seeking out the author. If they were talking about me, they had some things wrong. At the time I was sure one of my friends had given the reporter the information but soon learned the real truth from the author. The reporter from LifeSiteNews.com told me that the story was not about me at all. It was actually about another woman who was facing almost the exact same decision that I was.

Some of the comments on the article had quickly spun out of control, with many people accusing both me and the other woman of trying to scam people, saying we made up our stories. People soon found my Google account and I began to receive numerous hurtful emails. But I also got a lot of support, and I decided to start writing my blog again. I had not written a word since I went to Pennsylvania for my surrogate interview, so there was a lot that was missing.

I received a huge number of views after I published my first post. The nasty comments, along with those in support of my inclination to choose life, came in abundance. The first day was the hardest, reading the backlash from people who thought I should without question abort, and those who called me terrible names, making uncensored accusations about how I became a surrogate or why. Each one weighed on me and was instantly compounded when I received an email from Sharon confirming our meeting for the following day at a local bakery. Sharon's loyalties had never been clear and I was worried that she might threaten me in some way. She assured me over the phone that she simply wanted to talk and that she did not have any personal interests in the decision I made. I wanted to believe her, but in my heart I was still very nervous about meeting with her. I tried to call my mother but we kept missing each other. I went to bed that night, tossing and turning, unable to escape the nightmare.

FEBRUARY 13, 2012

I woke up feeling incredibly nauseous. I left the girls with my dad and ventured back towards the town where I had grown up. The mall was about a half hour drive away and I needed that time to clear my head and get my thoughts together. When I arrived and parked, I sat in my car for a few minutes, thinking about how my meeting with Sharon would go. I knew I had to get out of the car and find her, but it was taking all my energy to stop the panic attack that was slowly building in my chest. You weren't liking it either, Stormie, punching and kicking as I sat there trying to remain calm.

When I finally got out of the car I noticed a short blonde woman standing at the entrance to the bakery. She was nothing like I had expected, but was petite and slender with wispy fair hair and black wire-rimmed glasses. She had on an expensive looking jacket and a black bag with a gold chain for a strap. Under her arm were a number of file folders.

As I walked up to her she smiled. "Hi, Crystal. It's nice to finally meet you."

SAVING STORMIE: THE BABY S STORY

I had forgotten she had seen a picture of me during the application process. I had not been afforded the same advantage.

She motioned to the door. "This place looks a little busy. Why don't we go over there and have a sit down meal and chat." She pointed to a restaurant next door. It was quiet, with mood lighting and elevator music. We sat down and ordered some lunch.

"Get what ever you want," she said.

Still feeling very uncomfortable, I ordered a chicken salad and water.

We made idle chit-chat for a few minutes until our food came out, talking about my girls and how I had been feeling recently. I picked at the romaine lettuce, feeling the knot in my stomach grow larger and larger. When Sharon finished her small sandwich she folded her hands and looked at me.

"I know that this is very difficult for you. I want you to understand..." Sharon began.

I don't recall the specific words she used, Stormie, but her message was very clear. She tried to convince me to do what the Stones wanted me to do. She said that carrying a disabled child would bring great financial and emotional stress upon me and my family. She told me that the Stones did not want to have a disabled child and therefore, if I did not terminate, I would be responsible for your care after you were born. She emphasized that families with special-needs children often fall apart and said they endure terrible difficulties. She continued on, explaining that I shouldn't want that for my own family, and that I should spare myself and my daughters the pain of having to care for a special-needs baby.

I wanted her to stop talking. Yet, at the same time—and I hate to say this to you, Stormie—the things she was saying did make sense. With the influence that the comments in the online forums were having on me, I started to wonder if maybe giving in really was the best thing to do. I started to doubt my own conviction...

Could I really face the Stones in court if they decided to sue me for the financial part of the surrogacy?

Could I really handle the personal and financial ruin?

And what about my children? Did they deserve to be set aside while I moved forward in taking care of you, Stormie?

It all made my head spin.

"Crystal, the Stones feel awful about this. They know how hard this must be for you. It is not easy for them either. They know that you are financially in a tough spot, too. So they have authorized me to offer you an increase in the termination fee to ten thousand dollars. They will handle all the arrangements. You just need to show up for the procedure."

I was stunned. Ten thousand dollars? That was almost enough for me to be able to run away. I did not want to deal with this. I did not want to deal with a legal battle over monies put into the pregnancy. I did not want to deal with the personal struggle over how to care for another child. I did not want to hurt my daughters, and I did not want to hurt you, Stormie. I did not want to do any of it. But then maybe... just maybe... with ten thousand dollars, I argued, I could leave town. I could get up and take my kids and run away to a place where nobody knew me. I could start over and try to forget this had ever happened...

But I also knew that if I did abort, I would face a long struggle—an almost impossible struggle—to come back from a place of sadness and disappointment. I would not be able to work, and we would be starting over again. I didn't know if I could make it work for ten thousand, but an escape route had presented itself and was one that at the moment looked very appealing.

"I don't know if I can do it for that amount," I said at last, the words coming from I know not where.

As soon as I heard the words I felt my cheeks heating up, my heart-rate rising, my mind careering out of control. The words came from a stranger, certainly not from my own mouth.

"Tell me a number then," Sharon said quietly. "I'm sure we can make it happen."

I sat there for a few minutes, my mind now completely blank. She pushed a piece of paper and a pencil in front of me. I could not even see straight, but somehow I managed to take hold of the paper and write $15,000. I don't even know how I came up with the number, but I wrote it down and folded it in half before handing it back to her.

She nodded. "I think that will be okay."

"And a non-disclosure and no-contact order. I don't ever want to see them again."

As we walked out of the restaurant Sharon grabbed my elbow as if she was helping me down off the curb. The cold wind stung my face. I just wanted to get out of there, but she gripped my arm tightly and wouldn't let go.

"I'll find you another family, Crystal. You can still have a surrogacy. You can still have a baby. A healthy baby for a family."

I nodded. Somehow I found my keys and made it over to my car. The stinging of the wind left my cheeks and yet again I began to cry. I wrapped my hands around my belly and cried, saying over and over again, "I'm sorry, Stormie, I'm sorry, Stormie," at least twenty times. I cried so hard I could barely breathe. I sat in the parking lot for almost a half hour before I composed myself enough to drive away.

As I pulled into my driveway my mother called. Finally, we

could talk. She sounded calm as I answered the phone, but the tone quickly changed as I blurted out my news.

"Mom, I think I made a big mistake."

"What happened to our decision that you wouldn't talk to them until you and I got to talk?"

"There wasn't time. Sharon set up a meeting and I've just met with her. Mom, they offered me money to abort. I keep thinking maybe I should take it. I can't do this by myself. I don't have any money. I can barely pay my bills and I have two children to take care of. I don't know what to do. She said they can sue me. How can I go against that?"

"Okay. I'm sitting down now to look over the contract. I'll call you in an hour, okay?"

I walked into my house. It was eerily quiet. The girls were out with their father and I welcomed the time to think about everything without the constant commotion typically spinning around me.

I decided to check my email and saw I had a message from Sharon.

Crystal,

After speaking to you and to Roger and Ursula, I want to bring up the following clarifications:

In the present time you are in breach of the contract. It means the following:

1) The intended parents will stop paying monthly living support payments, effective immediately.

2) The intended parents did not file for the Parental Order, so

they will not be considered legal parents of the child, should the child be born.

3) You will be the only person who will be making decisions about the child, should the child be born.

In order to resolve the issue, Ursula and Roger present the following offer:

1) They agree to increase termination fee only to $10,000.

2) The fee will be paid in five installments: $2,000 at the day of termination with the remaining amount to be paid in installments, according with the statement prepared by their attorney.

3) They agree that both parties will sign a non-disclosure agreement, a no contact order, and a waiver of rights to sue or to bring the case to any court in the state of Connecticut and/or any other jurisdiction.

4) They will pay for the cost of termination.

If you accept this offer, please reply no later than Monday, February 19, 2012, 8 p.m. so that the intended parents can contact the clinic as early as 9 a.m., February 19, 2012.

My stomach did a flip-flop. Part of me was relieved. The amount they agreed to pay had not changed, so I did not feel any additional pressure. However, all the mixed feelings stemming from the previous meeting and the online reaction really had me questioning everything. I knew in my heart that I did not want to end the life that had been entrusted to me. I also knew that without the support of Ursula and Roger I could very easily lose my home, my stability, and possibly suffer other unforeseen consequences. A few close friends had already told me they would support me either way, and so I reached out to them. One told me to abort, another said she knew I would do the right thing. Only Kari, my doula, told me that no matter what I did she would be there with me.

I had no idea what I was going to do so I told Sharon I would keep her informed, and that I would let her know as soon as possible if I made an appointment at the clinic. The ten thousand dollars the Stones were offering was a large amount of money, and amidst all the chaos it seemed like an easy way to make a getaway. And at that moment I wanted nothing more than to run away from everything.

> To know what
> is right and
> not do it
> is the worst
> cowardice.
>
> —Confucius

CHAPTER SEVENTEEN
July 10, 2007

Greg had been my boyfriend for four years, and yet I **had never even met his parents.** It seemed like he didn't want anyone to know we were together. And now he had gotten some other girl pregnant.

"You've been trying to get away from this guy for how long now, Crystal?" the voice of my sister rang out in my head.

I knew she was right.

"I always thought I was special," I said. "Even when he messed around with other girls. He always came home to me."

"That doesn't make you special, Honey. That makes you his back-up. You deserve to be more than a back-up."

"I know," I said. "That's why I'm taking this trip. I'm going to get away from him once and for all. No more phone calls. No more begging to be paid attention to. I'm getting away and I'm never going back to it."

My bags were packed and my dad was waiting. As we drove past the billiards hall where I had met Greg I craned my neck to see if he was there. Sure enough, his beat up old blue car was sitting in the parking lot and he was standing outside, smoking a cigarette. Just the sight of him leaning up against the brick wall with his torn jeans and cocky expression made me want to scream.

"Dad, stop in here for a minute."

My father turned to face me, shook his head, and pulled in. He didn't say a word but I could tell by his usual disappointed grunt that he didn't approve of what I asked him to do.

I got out of the car and walked over to Greg, a piece of paper in my hand. As he looked up at me and smiled I glared back, jaw clenched, stomping my way towards him.

I said exactly what I had rehearsed in my head a million times.

"It's obvious to me that I don't really mean half of what you tell me I mean to you. I'm leaving. I hope you can figure out your life and how to be happy, but it'll have to be without me."

I put the folded-up piece of paper in his hand, and turned to walk away. I could hear him calling after me, but I kept walking and got in the car. "Let's go."

FEBRUARY 20, 2012

I never set out to become so public about such a private decision. I simply wanted to have a baby for a couple who couldn't have one themselves. All the joys of pregnancy without the personal commitment. I have a deep love for children. How could I possibly be against doing something that would bless another family with the gift of a child?

At the same time how could I deliberately end that life?

I wondered what lesson this was supposed to teach me and how I could possibly come out of this okay. I wished I could put Anne and Emmy in the car and drive away to a place so secluded and remote that no one would ever question our presence. Somewhere thousands of miles away, maybe even oceans, where no one knew who I was so I could start all over again.

Staring at the computer screen I closed out the surrogacy sites and reopened another window. In my email I had seen something come in from Veronica Ferris. I hoped she would have some answers to my questions.

Dear Crystal,

I am sorry but I will be unable to represent you. After we communicated, the intended parents came to our office and without my knowledge spoke to another lawyer in our firm. We now have a conflict of interest and we cannot legally represent any party to this problem. Please do your best to follow the doctors' advice and if you need a Connecticut attorney, I can send you the name of someone else in New Haven who may be able to help.

Veronica

That's great, I thought. Of course. *Just my luck.*

I thought about it for a minute or two longer. The author of one of the articles I had found online had mentioned something about a Defense of Life group who could possibly help. I sent off an email to the address I had been given and moments later I had the name and phone number of one of the head attorneys of the Allied Defense Fund, a national pro-bono defense of life firm. The firm was in Texas, but the attorney I spoke with quickly located someone closer. The emails and phone calls were piling up, and by the end of the day, I had an appointment to speak with a lawyer the next morning.

Later that day, I talked to my mother about the contract and together we wrote up a counter-offer. I had been scattered and confused when Sharon and I met, but this time I spelled it all out, leaving no question unanswered when it came to how I felt we should move forward. I did not believe for a minute that they would give me what I was about to ask for, and it was clear they were not going to increase the amount offered for termination to anything over $10,000. In order to keep my conscience clear, I needed to make an attempt to let the Stones change their mind.

At this time I cannot accept the offer. I am proposing a counter-offer to resolve the matter. Please forward this to them. Thank you, Sharon.

1) The intended parents will pay $10,000 to the gestational carrier who will not be getting an elective abortion and who will retain all legal, parental, and decision-making rights related to the child, unborn and born.

2) The fee will be paid in three installments by direct deposit into the bank account of the birth mother's choice. $5,000 will be deposited on the date the intended parents agree to this counteroffer. The remaining amount will be paid in monthly installments of $2,500 due on the first day of April 2012, and

$2,500 due on the first day of May 2012. Payments continue to be due even if the child dies, is born, or has any other change in circumstances.

3) In exchange for this, the gestational carrier agrees with the intended parents that both parties will sign a non-disclosure statement, a no contact order, and a waiver of rights to sue or to bring the case to any court in the state of Connecticut or New York and/or any other jurisdiction. There will also be an affidavit or agreement stating that the "Gestational Surrogacy Agreement" is null and void and the intended parents no longer desire to assume any parental rights or obligations to the child born to the gestational carrier through the named agreement and will not be taking custody of the child. As well as an affidavit or agreement stating that the gestational carrier accepts full responsibility for the child and will not pursue child support or anything else from the intended parents as reviewed and approved by the gestational carrier's legal counsel.

4) The intended parents must immediately direct deposit payment of travel and childcare expenses in the amount of $220 due the birth mother, up to and including the day of February 16, 2012.

5) This offer is null and void if not accepted, in writing, from the intended parents by Friday, February 24, 2012 at 6 p.m. To accept this offer the gestational carrier requests a printed, signed, and dated copy of this email be scanned and returned via email to this email address.

If the intended parents agree to this offer they may sign and date below:

> We agree to the terms of this offer and consider the matter resolved and the Gestational Surrogacy Agreement is null and void.

It was getting late and I wondered where Scott was with the girls. We had been getting along pretty well over the last few weeks, and he had said he was going to stay and watch a movie with me. Shortly afterwards, I heard his tires grinding up my gravel driveway.

The girls were asleep in the backseat. As I unbuckled Emmy, Scott hoisted Anne onto his shoulder. We hauled them up the stairs and into bed before plopping down on the couch. I was getting too big to carry even little Emmy up the stairs without getting out of breath and felt exhaustion take over my body.

"How was your day?" Scott asked, slumping into the couch next to me. I took a deep breath in, leaning towards him as I inhaled his cologne. I missed the way he smelled.

"Exhausting. I've talked to the agent, a journalist, two lawyers, and my mother. I feel like I've been running all day."

"So have you made a decision?"

"I think so. I mean, I'm pretty sure I'm keeping her."

"Are you serious?" His reaction surprised me.

"Of course I'm serious. Did you really think I was going to be able to abort and be okay?"

"I don't understand how you think you can have this baby and keep it," Scott said, pulling away from me.

"Well, they're clearly not interested in raising her. What else am I supposed to do?"

"And who is going to take care of her, Crystal? You have two children of your own. I'm not going to be supporting all of you. I'm not saying that I don't understand why you want to do this, but I hope you don't think that it's all going to be just fine if you keep this baby. Think of what that'd mean for our kids. We didn't sign up for this. I didn't sign up for this. This was your idea. I don't want our kids to suffer because of a decision that you made."

"I know. But I can't let that be the reason I don't give this baby a chance."

My phone rang. It was my mom. "I'm answering this, Scott."

He looked away, angry, but I answered it anyway. I needed to talk to my mother more than I needed to fight with him.

"Did you send the counter-offer?" she asked.

"Yeah. Sharon's forwarding it to the Stones."

"Do you know what you're going to do?"

Yet again I began to cry. All I seemed to be doing for the last few days was cry. "No, Mom. I don't. I don't know how I'm going to do this without any income. I can't exactly stay in a rental for free, and I sure as hell can't get a job right now. How am I going to keep my kids safe? How am I supposed to survive?"

"Crystal. You have to stop thinking about the little stuff. Make the big decisions and deal with the little ones when they come. You need to think about what this is going to do to you mentally. Are you going to be okay going through all this again?"

With those words, Stormie, my world came crashing down. It felt as if someone had turned out the lights and put the world on mute. *What is the date? Did I miss it? February 20th. I can't believe it.* Like a ton of bricks it struck me. I missed my first child's birth/death date. My little girl, so wanted and so loved. My beautiful sweet girl born too soon. How was this little girl inside me any different? You were older in gestation, Stormie, than my Miranda had been. You were feisty and active, which Miranda had not been. There were only two differences: Miranda was biologically mine; and with her I didn't have a choice. The genetics of the child didn't matter when it came to matters of life and death, I decided. How would I be able to live with myself or look at myself in the mirror, knowing that when I had been given the choice, I chose to deny life to a child? How would I continue to exist having to mourn the loss of two babies both in the month of February; one which I lost at the fault of no one, and one which I consciously chose to kill?

Who would I become if I took a life away from the most helpless of all—the unborn? Would I be able to tell myself she's too little? She would have died anyway? How could I, Stormie? The perils that come with being frozen for years, thawing, implanting, and then developing into a baby; she overcame every one of those, even with her limitations and her developing abnormalities. A life force that strong cannot live without a purpose. Who was I to say that the life inside that child was not worth giving her a chance? How could I, Stormie?

I stared at Scott as I held the phone up to my ear. "I can't," I said. "I can't kill her. She deserves a chance to have a life. I can't take that away. It's not my decision to make."

"And Crystal," my mother added. "I think you should consider letting someone else raise her. We don't have to decide that now, but it's something we should think about."

I knew she was right, so while Scott found a movie to watch, I went online to Facebook and posted in a couple of different places.

Despite our argument earlier, Scott and I snuggled together on the couch, his arm around me while I rested my head on his shoulder. His silence told me he didn't want to fight anymore. He knew he wouldn't win this battle.

After the movie was over I struggled with the decision to

go to bed since there was so much I could be doing. But it was late, and I had another busy day ahead of me, so I dragged myself into my bedroom and put on my Hypnobabies CD. The soothing music calmed my racing thoughts, and I think you liked it too, Stormie, because even you settled more quickly when it played. For the first time in days, I slept well.

My phone rang at 8 a.m. I jumped up, startled to be woken so early. Scott was gone, and both Emmy and Anne were curled up at the foot of my bed. Groggy, I reached to silence the ringing.

"Hello?"

Good morning. Crystal Kelley?"

"Yes..."

"Crystal, this is Michael DePrimo. I'm with the Allied Defense League. How are you?"

"Umm. Awake. I think."

Michael laughed. "I'm sorry. Did I wake you? I'll tell you what, Crystal. Let me get some information from you and we can meet up sometime in the next couple of days and have a talk about what's going on. Does that sound good? I'm sure you're anxious to get some answers about the legal end of all this."

Anxious was exactly how I felt, and disturbed, and uneasy, and every other word I could think of to describe the tension gripping my mind and my body. He rattled off a few different things he wanted me to send him: the contract, a copy of all the emails, and a synopsis of all interactions between myself, the agency and the intended parents. As I scrambled for a pen we set an appointment to meet the following morning at a diner down the road.

"Is it okay if I bring my kids?" I asked.

"Of course" he said. "I love kids."

CHAPTER SEVENTEEN

When I finally did get out of bed that day, the first thing I did was check my email. The greatly anticipated response to my counter-offer was waiting in my inbox.

Please confirm if you will or will not be scheduling the appointment for termination.

By that point I had made up my mind, Stormie. I wasn't going to stand by and let someone else make decisions for me. I truly felt that you deserved a chance. You were so fragile, with such big odds against you, and yet you were living inside me, your heart beating alongside mine, defect and all.

I gathered up every bit of my courage and hit Reply. One word, two letters, that's all it took. I hit Send and forwarded a copy to attorney DePrimo.

I had officially said 'No.'

■ ■ ■

Feeling as though I had a weight lifted from my shoulders I went off with my family for the day. We did fun things, like walking through the field where the flowers were starting to bud. It was warm for February in Connecticut, but I was grateful for that. I had never been one of those pregnant women who was hot all the time. My internal heater was permanently broken, so I was thankful for the glowing sun.

After a day in the fresh air we took a trip to the grocery store. We were loading everything into the car and getting ready to go home when I got a phone call from a number I did not recognize. Since I had been talking to so many new people, I answered the phone.

The local sheriff was on the line. He had a letter for me. My heart sank and I started to sweat. I felt as if my worst fears were about to come true. I didn't want to go home and get that letter, but the sheriff assured me I wasn't being served; it was just a letter. I drove home feeling panicked, and accepted it in the dark driveway adjacent to my house. When I got upstairs, I quickly scanned the letter.

Dear Ms. Kelley:

I represent Roger and Ursula Stone in matters related to a Gestational Surrogacy Agreement, a contract executed by you on September 1, 2011, and by Mr. and Mrs. Stone on September 2, 2011. If you are represented by counsel please forward this letter to him or her immediately.

On or about October 8, 2011, you underwent an in-vitro fertilization procedure which resulted in the implantation of an embryo and your becoming pregnant under the Gestational Surrogacy Agreement. On February 13, 2012 you underwent a sonogram of the fetus, which detected abnormalities with the fetus. On February 16, 2012, you underwent a further sonographic examination at Hartford Hospital, which detected multiple fetal abnormalities, including complex cardiac defects, an absent stomach and a cleft lip. Your doctor stated that this was a 'very complicated pregnancy.'

Paragraph 8 on page 5 of the Gestational Surrogacy Agreement states: Abortion and Selective Reduction due to severe fetus abnormality: The Gestational Carrier agrees to selective fetus reduction or/and abortion in case of severe fetus abnormality as determined by 3-dimentional [sic] ultrasound test with following pathology expertise or by any other procedure or test(s) used to diagnose severe fetus abnormality.

Since the date of the Hartford Hospital sonograph and associated consultation, my clients have repeatedly informed you that they wish the pregnancy to be terminated in accordance with the terms of the contract. On Tuesday, February 21, 2012, your surrogacy agent asked whether you were scheduling an appointment for termination of this pregnancy. Your emailed answer was one word: 'No.'

Pursuant to the terms of the Gestational Surrogacy Agreement, specifically the above-referenced Paragraph 8, due to severe fetus abnormalities you are obligated to terminate this pregnancy immediately. TIME IS OF THE ESSENCE. You are expected to reach your 24th week of pregnancy on or about March 5, and the abortion must take place before that date. By refusing to honor and abide by the terms of your contract, you have squandered precious time. Because of this, your response to this letter must be received in writing by me no later than 3 p.m. on Friday, February 24, 2012.

Persuant to Paragraph 9 on page 5 of the Gestational Surrogacy Agreement, Mr. and Mrs. Stone shall pay you the required $2,000 fee due to the termination of this pregnancy because of severe fetus abnormality, which shall be payable upon the termination of the pregnancy. Any and all other offers are hereby rescinded.

We fully expect you to abide by and comport with the terms of your contract with Mr. and Mrs. Stone. Should you fail to honor the terms of this contract, you shall be in breach, and we shall pursue every legal means of recovery, including demands for specific performance according to the terms of the contract, along with the return of all monies paid for all expenses incurred on your behalf by Mr. and Mrs. Stone, including (but not limited to) agency fees, pre-transfer medical treatment fees, laboratory fees, medications, doctors' fees, embryo transfer fees, fees paid to your surrogacy agency, medical insurance costs, living expenses and transportation expenses, legal fees, and other associated losses.

I look forward to hearing from you.

I immediately called attorney DePrimo, then emailed the letter to him.

Two minutes later my phone rang.

"This changes things," attorney DePrimo said upon opening the email I had forwarded. "Don't respond to it. Don't contact anyone involved with this matter. Consider me officially retained as your lawyer and we will discuss where to go from here when I see you in the morning."

■　■　■

The next morning when I woke up, I hoped Michael was truly as fond of children as he said he was. My girls were feisty little things, and they were rarely seen sitting still before 2 p.m. At 10 a.m. they were ready for action, and were quickly bored with the coloring page and crayons provided by the diner staff. Over their incessant bouncing we discussed the legality of the case and Mr. DePrimo admitted he knew very little about surrogacy law, but was passionate about constitutional law and first amendment rights.

"The right to life," he explained, "is comparable to free

speech. It is the freedom to make decisions and choices regarding your own person."

Even the most commonly quoted pro-choice law, Roe v. Wade, guaranteed that I could not be forced to abort. The implications of that were unknown at the time, but attorney DePrimo promised to look into it as quickly as possible. As per the Allied Defense Fund, I signed an affidavit declining any interest in terminating the pregnancy, and other paperwork legally retaining Michael as my lawyer. I told him everything, Stormie, even the guilt I felt over my previous statement saying I would abort for even more money, which thankfully was ignored. When he asked me why I did it, I told him I was so blindsided by the discussion of the agent that I didn't know what else to tell her.

"As long as you're sure now," he said. "Whatever you did then doesn't matter. It's what you actually do now that counts."

■　■　■

When I got home, Michael and I drew up a response letter to the Stones' attorney's letter and sent it off. Now there was nothing left to do but wait. At least, on the legal end of things. But I still had to figure out how I would get my medical care taken care of, and how I was going to keep myself afloat financially over the next few months. I had a few ideas, but no long-term plan in place. I was going to have to figure out something though, and fast.

> The gem
> cannot be
> polished without
> friction, nor
> man perfected
> without trials.
>
> —Chinese Proverb

CHAPTER EIGHTEEN
March 2, 2012

It took what seemed like forever, Stormie, for everything to fall into place. I was twenty-one weeks pregnant when your issues were first identified, and over the next three weeks we raced to secure insurance, went back and forth with the lawyers, and struggled over the decisions concerning how I was going to continue to care for the rest of my family without the monthly deposit from the Stones.

The insurance became a really big issue. Thanks to my complete disclosure with the midwives' office, I was ineligible for Medicaid for Pregnant Women. This meant that I could keep my Medicaid Family insurance, but I could not use it for anything related to the pregnancy. At the same time, the status of the surrogacy contract prohibited me from obtaining any other coverage. We knew you were going to require a number of tests and the costs leading up to your delivery could be extravagant. While this was a huge underlying problem, the most pressing matter was finding out exactly what was happening inside your little body so that we could make sound decisions about what path we were going to take for your care. Luckily my mother offered to pay for the first fetal echo.

We needed a referral to get into the best hospital around—Yale—so I had to jump through several hoops to obtain access. I had to become a patient at Hartford Hospital's maternity clinic, have an examination, and secure my official due date. I also had to have another Level Two ultrasound before they would even send me the paperwork. I couldn't believe it, Stormie. When it was all over I had seen four different doctors just to get a referral to the hospital where I intended to have you.

I had copies of all my records and read over them from time to time. But this time, as I sat at my kitchen table, something struck me as odd. I found a note stating that Ursula had called the genetic counselor several times after the initial ultrasound to get more information about your diagnosis. She had also requested referrals for specialists. If Roger and Ursula were not interested in caring for you after your birth, why was Ursula interested in what your prognosis was?

At the same time, Michael was making some legal discoveries that were very concerning:

In doing further legal research, I have discovered that under Connecticut law a gestational carrier that is biologically unrelated to the child has no parental rights with respect to that child. Therefore, the legal parents of the child you are carrying are Roger and Ursula.

I wrote an email back:

Is there a way, through arbitration or agreement, to offer them
to relinquish their parental rights? I would much rather take
responsibility myself and remove them from the picture so that
this baby can have a chance at a life with a family that wants
and loves her, not one that sees her as a burden that was forced
upon them. Those situations never end up in the baby's best
interests.

He responded:

In Connecticut, there are only three ways to acquire parental
rights: Through: 1) biological relationship, 2) adoption, or 3)
artificial insemination. The Supreme Court has expressly stated
that so-called gestational carriers have no parental rights. Once
the baby is born and outside of your body, you no longer have
any right or power to make decisions affecting the baby. Only a
court can award or terminate parental rights; it cannot be done
through arbitration or agreement.

I haven't heard from the intended parents' lawyer and I've
considered writing him to ask, in effect, if they intend to comply
with their parental responsibilities as the biological parents.
However, my thinking is that such a pointed question might
provoke a negative response and do more harm than good.
Therefore, at this time I'm inclined to remain silent unless
you instruct me to declare them in breach of contract for the
purpose of seeking immediate financial relief (which is a long
shot). My recommendation is that, for now, we do nothing.

Here's a possible scenario: If we and the intended parents do nothing for the next several months we can, 30-60 days before your due date, notify the Department of Children and Families that the baby is about to be born. (Because you have no parental rights you cannot offer the baby up for adoption.) Upon birth the Department of Children and Families will take custody of the baby and be responsible for her care. They will then place the baby in foster care and file suit to terminate the intended parents' parental rights (by refusing to provide for the baby they are unfit parents). Once the intended parents' parental rights are terminated, the baby will be put up for adoption. Under this scenario you are out of the picture with respect to the baby upon birth. It is also possible that the intended parents might file suit themselves to have their parental rights terminated.

Notwithstanding the above, because we are plowing new legal ground, nothing is for certain.

The news was disconcerting to say the least and a couple of days later, after it had all sunk in, my unhappiness turned to anger. I received a phone call from Michael, stating that he had spoken to the lawyer representing Roger and Ursula. They had proposed a solution.

"Connecticut has what's called a Safe Haven law," Michael said. "According to this, parents can drop off a newborn child within the first thirty days of his or her life at any police department or hospital without fear of prosecution. The Stones have proposed that you sign an affidavit affirming that you are aware that they will be placing her into state custody by right of that law."

"What?" I screamed.

Upon hearing my eruption of disgust, Scott looked over at me. "What's wrong?"

Still holding the phone up to my ear, I began to get increasingly agitated, and so were you, Stormie, kicking and thumping in my belly. "They want me to give her to the state. I can't have her, so they want to give her away to whoever happens to get stuck with her in state custody!"

"What do you mean?" Scott looked as confused as I felt, his brow scrunched up and furrowed.

I continued into the phone. "They want to let her be born and then throw her away. I can't stand this. I'm supposed to protect this baby, and then, once she's born, if Roger and Ursula don't come and take her home, then she's going to go into state custody and I'll never see her again. And I'm supposed to hand them this baby and hope that they won't screw up taking care of her. No. No way. I am not willing to accept that. There has to be another way. All the horror stories of kids who get lost or abused in the system and I'd have no way to even find out what happened to her. I can't let that happen."

I realized I was yelling, but I didn't care anymore. I had seen the state child protective services at work with some of my friends' kids; my niece and nephew had recently been handed back to their abusive father over a concern for the number of bedrooms in my sister's current living situation. Another friend had experienced her children being removed from the home because of a drunk grandmother who provided them with shelter. There were worse stories on the news about caregivers being charged with abusing the children in their care, and horror stories from children in foster care. I would not be responsible for allowing another child to enter the system only to slip through the cracks, as children with special needs easily could.

"I can't believe this," I said to Michael. "Let me calm down and I'll call you later."

CHAPTER EIGHTEEN

■ ■ ■

It was three years since I had left the house of Julie and the Alvarez kids. Those three little blondies—the kids I had taken care of for an entire year while their mother was out doing drugs and whatever else she did—it was as if they were my own, and yet when it came to making sure they were safe, I had failed. People in the neighborhood said Julie had packed up the kids and moved them to Mexico when I had called protective services, reporting her for nearly burning the baby while she was getting high. The minute the report was made, I lost them. I was kicked out, and my mother had picked up my belongings from the house a few days later. I had lost a lot of really valuable stuff, but I wasn't worried about my possessions. My heart ached for those kids. Little Jeralee had been only a year old and I wondered where she was now.

During my rage, I decided to test the system. I called the number of the worker who had taken my report back then. Somehow, even after all these years I still had her card.

"Dominica Revalo," she answered.

"Hi, I'm not sure if you remember me, but I made a report a few years ago. I was wondering if there was any way I could find out what happened in the case against Julie Alvarez."

"I'm sorry, all client cases are confidential. I can't give you any information."

"Not even if they are still in the system? Can you just tell me if they're okay?"

"I'm sorry."

I hung up the phone and dropped my head into my hands, my body quivering as I held back tears. *You could end up the same way, Stormie.* I walked into the living room and sat down on the couch, watching my stomach move as you kicked and punched. "I don't want to be forced to let you go," I said out loud to you. "I refuse to give you up this way. Screw the Safe Haven law." Tears gathered in the corners of my eyes as I stared up at the ceiling. "Please tell me what I'm supposed to do," I said into the air.

I got up, walked into the kitchen and grabbed my computer from the counter, taking it with me to the table. After turning it on, I logged into my Facebook fan page and vented my feelings to the group, telling them what Roger and Ursula had intended to do with you after you were born. My hands shook as my fingers tapped on the keyboard, so much that I could barely type the details. Within seconds, several people had responded and were as outraged as I was. 'How do they expect you to carry this child then give her up and walk away?' one woman said.

I had always assumed that I would continue to know you long after your birth. It was something Roger, Ursula and I had discussed at length. With their new proposition, none of us would see you grow up. My friends online and I agreed that they were grasping at straws to regain control of the situation, but there were also concerns that because of where we were, there existed the possibility of the State of Connecticut making some type of legal determination that would make their suggestion concrete.

■　■　■

A couple of days later, I was out getting the mail when my phone rang. Michael was on the line. "I just wanted to check on you," he said. "How are you doing?"

I opened the driver's side door to my car, but remained sitting inside in order to escape the windy March weather. "Okay, I guess. I can't believe there is not *any* way I can make sure that this baby is safe after she's born. I mean, I would take care of her, but I don't know that I'll be able to. The letter from the agent said that she would become my responsibility and that's what I was banking on. I don't want her to go to the state, and the intended parents have made it very clear that they do not want to be involved at all."

"Well, Crystal, I was looking over the contract and something occurred to me. I wasn't sure, which is why I didn't call you right away, but I've checked with the other Defense of Life attorneys and we've agreed that there may be another option for you."

The silence as I waited for him to continue was deafening. "Yes?" I whispered.

"Well, the contract says a lot of things about where the court proceedings should take place, if they happen. But it doesn't say anywhere in here that you have to stay in Connecticut."

"What does that mean?"

"As we've discussed before, Connecticut state law does not allow you to obtain parental rights. That isn't the case everywhere, though. If you lived in, say, New York, then the surrogacy agreement wouldn't be allowed in court, which would mean that the intended parents would have to fight for parental rights. There are a number of states in the USA that have declared surrogacy agreements to be void of public policy. In those states, the woman who gives birth to the child is declared the child's legal mother."

"You're suggesting I leave?"

"Not suggesting," he clarified quickly. "But it could be a possibility."

> Hope is important because it can make the present moment less difficult to bear. If we believe that tomorrow will be better, we can bear a hardship today.
>
> —Thich Nhat Hanh

"Crystal Kelley?"

I looked up to see a nurse standing in the doorway. She held a file in her hands packed full of papers. It did not seem small enough to be mine; I had only begun my prenatal care at the practice ten weeks ago. Then again, in those short ten weeks I had already seen four different doctors and had several ultrasounds.

"Yup," I said, pushing myself up out of the chair to a standing position. My mother, who had been sitting next to me, gathered my bag as well as her purse.

It was growing harder and harder to move as my belly expanded. I was twenty-four weeks along and just into my seventh month. Physically I felt fabulous, Stormie, but mentally I had burned out every fiber of acceptance and understanding I could muster. I no longer had the energy to fight with Roger and Ursula about your existence but I knew I had to trudge through the thick mud, oceans deep, to get through whatever lay ahead and make it through to the other side.

I was scheduled for a fetal echo, and then a follow-up with pediatric cardiology to discuss the findings. The doctor who did the echo was quite the character. He entered the room wearing a purple jacket and matching spotted bow tie, his hair mussed in the center on top of his head.

"You're going to hear us use a lot of very technical terms," Dr. Cohen said. "At the end I'll explain exactly what we're seeing so that you can understand it all."

He didn't realize my mother was a nurse. I had a hard time following what he talked about but I could tell my mother was listening very carefully. She had a little notebook, and every once in a while she would jot something down. Her notes made more sense to me than trying to listen to what the doctors were saying, although there were some things I did understand. Now and again he would say something comedic between technical discussions, and smile and wink at me.

He even talked to you through my belly, and told you that your feistiness would serve you well in life.

When he was done, he leaned on the side of the ultrasound machine as if it were a podium. "Okay, so here's what we're seeing. This baby does in fact have a stomach. There is no blockage to the stomach, it's just in the wrong place. I always say, if the stomach isn't on the right side, look on the left. Sure enough, her stomach is right here." He pointed to the image on the screen. "What this indicates is a condition called *situs* inversus which is otherwise known as 'Ivemark Syndrome,' or 'heterotaxy.' Basically, *situs inversus* means that the sides are switched. The organs that are supposed to be on the right side of the body are on the left. Now in the case of *situs inversus totalis* the implications are minimal. There is a mirror image development where all the organs are in the exact opposite spots. Many older individuals who have this type of heterotaxy are completely unaware of it. Unfortunately, it seems as though your baby has what we call *situs inversus ambiguous*. The organs are not all in their exact opposite spots, in fact they are quite often in random places. The bad news is that this type of placement often indicates a number of other problems. There is a chance of intestinal malrotation as well as several different heart issues going on. And of course there is the cleft as well. I'm not going to lie—her heart is very complicated. What I'd like to do is send this over to our pediatric cardiologist before your appointment on Thursday so that she can take a look and have a little advance prep time to be able to tell you exactly what she sees in the heart, and what that will mean for the baby's prognosis."

He was very straightforward, no nonsense.

"Where do you think she would be able to get the best care after birth?" I asked. His response was not what I had expected.

"Well, typically I would tell you that Yale's facilities would be well suited, but the truth is that we are a very small hospital in comparison to some. For the best care, you want to be in a cardiac center that sees this type of child often. Yale certainly has the capability, but your prognosis may be better if you were to deliver in a place that has more experience with complex cardiac defects. I would definitely say that you want to have this baby in a place where you have access to one of the top ten cardiac hospitals. If you were to stay here you would have access to Boston or New York hospitals, both of which are very good choices."

Before he left the room, he told me that he had no doubt you were one of the stronger sick babies he had ever dealt with.

I went home with some answers, Stormie, but still a lot of questions. What was the prognosis for your survival through the pregnancy? Should I stay at Yale or go elsewhere? What was going to happen after birth? Would you need immediate care? Would you live past infancy?

As soon as I got home, I opened up my computer and logged in. I needed some answers. A quick Google search brought up links from WebMD and Wikipedia on Ivemark Syndrome. They didn't give me much information, though. I searched for *situs inversus* and the number of hits grew. As I scrolled down, I noticed a link for The Congenital Heart Information Network. Determined to get more information I clicked on their webpage and searched the site. I got a little information and links to various Facebook pages. Since Facebook had always given me the resources I needed, I clicked on the link. It brought me to the Facebook page for the Congenital Heart Information Network, so I 'liked' it.

A few days later, my mother and I made the trek back out to Yale. This time we were accompanied by my biological sister, Bethany, and both my children. Bethany sat in a narrow hallway with Emmy and Anne while we met with a short, dark-haired woman in a tiny office. The appointment had been made last minute so the location was not where the cardiologist typically saw people. Her office was cluttered, and she moved several files in order to make room for the two of us to sit.

"Hi, Crystal. I'm Doctor McDonald. We have a lot to discuss so I will get started."

Dr. McDonald showed me the picture of a normal heart. She

explained its function and then she took out another piece of paper.
"It was very difficult to find a proper picture to describe what I'm seeing from the echo that Dr. Cohen gave me. I actually ended up making my own, so please excuse my horrible drawing skills."

The picture she showed us was similar to those I had seen in my research, but at the same time completely different. As she explained, you had a large hole in the middle of your heart. There was an atrioventricular septal defect, a ventricular septal defect, an interrupted inferior vena cava, malposition of the great arteries, pulmonary stenosis, pulmonary venous return to a right sided atrium, and a right-sided aortic arch. All these things were different from what they would expect to see in a normal heart.

Dr. McDonald handed me her drawing, with notes filling up the entire page, wrapping around almost every inch of the perimeter. Twelve different abnormalities in all.

My mother broke the silence. "What does this mean for the baby after it is born?"

The doctor explained that in her opinion your heart was not developed enough to be surgically corrected all at once. You would need a minimum of two, perhaps three, heart operations to create a single ventricle heart. There was about a sixty to sixty-five percent mortality rate within the first year for heterotaxy.

If you survived the first year, your prognosis would be much better. With a single ventricle heart, you would not be able to play sports or be as active as other children but you could still live a very full life.

I knew this, Stormie. I had already started receiving emails from individuals who were survivors of congenital heart defects, and several single ventricle heart patients had come forward to show their support. Still, it was all so complicated. There was a fifty-fifty shot that you would need your first surgery within days of birth, and a minimum of two other operations. Adding in all the other complications, such as the possible abdominal malrotation and the cleft, I began to wonder if, for your sake, little one, I had made the right choice.

Dr. McDonald must have noticed a change in my demeanor. She leaned forward and whispered, "Honey. Usually I meet with people long before their twenty-fourth week so that they can make the choice of whether or not to terminate. I can see that this is not an option for you. I just want you to know I really believe that children are a blessing, and if you feel that this baby has a strong spirit, then your instincts are right on. We see these babies fairly infrequently, but I can tell you that the tenacious ones, the ones with the toughest spirits always do the best. I've seen her on ultrasound and I can tell you that she is one of the tough ones. Stay strong for her. It's all you can do now."

■　■　■

Driving away from the clinic my mother suggested that we stop at Ikea. There was only one Ikea in the whole state and we happened to be a few blocks away. I was in a daze, and so I agreed. We had lunch at the store and the girls ran around with Bethany. My mother stayed with me for most of our time there. At one point we caught the girls jumping on one of the demo beds in the store. As they ran off, giggling, my mother looked at me. "Would you love them any less if one of them was in a wheelchair, or if they weren't quite so active?"

"Less activity would probably make it more enjoyable," I replied, smiling. I was beginning to feel okay again. I wandered through the bargain aisle, hoping to find something for the girls to play with. Our apartment was small but I could still fit in the perfect piece if I found it. In one of the bargain bins, just as we were getting ready to leave, was a small purple journal with a silver tree etched on it. Something about it drew me in, made me think of you, Stormie.

"Mom, can I get this?" I asked.

She looked at it and smiled. "Of course, it's perfect."

I stared at the purple book the entire ride home, loving the freshness of the clean blank pages and suddenly knowing what I would write in them. The tree was etched into the cover, it's stark metallic silver standing bright against the contrasting background color. It looked like a strong tree; the tree of life. I believed in signs and remember thinking to myself, *I'm the strong tree in this storm.*

And you were my storm.

It was from that day forward that I started calling you Stormie.

> To go against the dominant thinking of your friends, of most of the people you see every day, is perhaps the most difficult act of heroism you can perform.
>
> —Theodore H. White

CHAPTER TWENTY
March 22, 2012

"**W**hat do you want to do?" My mother's voice rang out from the other end of the telephone. Her voice faded in and out, as it always did in my house with our scrambled connection. My heart was pounding, knowing the decision I had made would alter many lives.

"I want to get out of here, Mom. I can't do this here. I can't let this kid be born and then lose her forever. I just... I don't know how I'm going to do it."

"Well, start looking," she said. "You at least want to know what your options are."

I logged into my Facebook account. The group I had created grew larger by the day with several people wishing me the best of

luck, showing sincere concern for me and the girls. Every one of
the people in the group had been asked to join by another member.
I didn't allow unsolicited invites. The members of the group were
from all over the United States, and even some overseas. They
responded immediately with information for me, as well as a few
different offers of places to stay if I decided to relocate to their city or
town. I was absolutely overwhelmed with the response from people
I knew, and even the strangers who only knew *of* me.

Through the Congenital Heart Information Network I
was able to find a link to the Heterotaxy Network, and connected
directly with its owner, the mother of a little boy with heterotaxy.
She raved about Boston Children's Hospital, and I started thinking
seriously about Massachusetts. Michael told me that the laws were
shaky there and that there had not been a ruling on surrogacy on
the books. I didn't want to be the first.

I looked into what the top hospitals were in the United States
for pediatric cardiology and who had experience with heterotaxy.
Both Dr. Cohen and Dr. McDonald had given us their top choices for
hospitals if we chose to continue care somewhere other than Yale.
'U.S. News' published a handy article written about the top pediatric
cardiology hospitals, and according to that report, three of the top
five hospitals in the U.S. were Boston Children's Hospital, a hospital
in Pennsylvania, and Mott's Children's Hospital in Michigan.

Michael wasn't aware of the laws in many of these states
since he wasn't a surrogacy lawyer. However, he compiled a list of
all possible states, discussing over many phone conversations the
pros and cons of each one in great detail.

In the end Missouri seemed like the best option. I knew
people there and I really thought I would have the best chance of
success staying somewhere I was familiar with and where I had

resources in the community. Michigan and Florida were also legally and medically beneficial, with good hospitals and laws stating that surrogacy contracts were void of public policy. These states had documented case history in which surrogates gained parental rights of a child who was not biologically theirs.

Michael sent me the names and contact information for a Defense of Life affiliated lawyer in each state. I did my own search and sent off a few emails to narrow down my options. The individuals Michael had found seemed to be very busy. We received several responses stating that they were too swamped to add my case to their already towering workload. However, one of the emails I sent out elicited some results.

John Mills, a Defense of Life lawyer in Michigan, had a name for me. He sent contact information to both me and Michael for an attorney named Herb Brail. The following day Michael called me. He had already spoken to Mr. Brail and wanted to schedule a conference call so we could all talk. He said he was very optimistic about Michigan after speaking with the attorney about the situation.

The next day, just before one of my weekly appointments, I sat in a parking lot down the street and got on a conference call with Michael and Mr. Brail.

Mr. Brail's voice was light and hopeful. This was exciting, Stormie. He sounded like someone with confidence in his words and clearly had experience with assisted reproduction. He was a lifelong adoption attorney and many of the laws that applied to surrogacy were ones he had written or assisted in writing. He felt positive, that without the Stones' involvement, we would be able to move forward with the intention of protecting you by allowing you to be born in Michigan.

"We have a wonderful Children's hospital in Ann Arbor

and you will be safe from being prosecuted by anyone looking to
get anything from you as a result of the surrogacy contract. The
biological parents would have to prove their parentage, and even if
they were successful in doing so they would only have half of the
parental rights. In the state of Michigan the legal mother of a child is
the woman who gives birth to the child."

"So what about custody? Would I be able to give the child up
for adoption or would they need to consent?"

"Well, to do things the easy way we would probably ask
them to terminate their rights, but with what I've heard from your
attorney it doesn't seem as if they have any intention of pursuing
custody. If they don't want custody, then establishing parentage is
pointless."

I sat quietly in the car for a few minutes and listened as the
two lawyers set out a plan for your future. They were discussing
legal terms I barely understood. After a while, I interjected. "So
basically there is not really any way I can lose by going to Michigan.
If the Stones come after me for custody then, as the legal mother, I
have a say. If they don't, then I can give her up for adoption? And
they can't come after me for any money since the contract isn't
admissible. Do I have that right?"

"Absolutely," Mr. Brail said. "Sounds like you are a smart
girl. You've got it absolutely right."

We ended our conversation with the promise that we would
be in touch in the next few days to let Mr. Brail know our decision.
I was still not thoroughly convinced Michigan was the right choice.
It was not a place I was familiar with and I wondered where I
would live and how I would manage financially, alone with my two
daughters. I did not have any family or friends there, and the reality
that I would have to house and support my two children while we

were there weighed heavily on me.

It was really difficult, Stormie. Just as with the decision of whether or not to terminate the pregnancy had consumed me, the decision to move away and continue my maternity care elsewhere was not something I could quickly determine. I felt a tremendous amount of guilt in taking my children away from what we had grown to think of as our home, and I knew the journey would be difficult. I would have to break my lease, figure out housing, and somehow manage to take my daughters hundreds of miles away where we had no one and no money to get us there. Beyond moving, I also knew that Roger and Ursula were angry about my decision to give birth to you. I envisioned them showing up one day on my doorstep, demanding I change my mind. I didn't know what they could actually do, but I still lived in fear of having a direct confrontation with them.

The communication between Roger, Ursula, and me had been strictly through our lawyers. They had not reached out to Michael for anything other than the dates and times of my appointments and he didn't offer the addresses of where I would be, but stated that they should let us know if they wanted to attend any of the doctor's visits and, if so, he would provide them with the information they needed. Still, the Stones showed no interest in coming to any of my appointments. Even though I felt relieved that they didn't come, it made me sad to know they had given up on you, Stormie, someone they had said they wanted so much.

The stress of the situation had taken over every part of me. I couldn't sleep and dark circles had formed under my eyes, revealing my exhaustion. Often, the only person I would speak openly to about my feelings was my counselor, Christina.

I had been seeing her since the surrogacy process began.

Very aware of my own emotional background, I had sought her out for an unbiased opinion. She reigned in my emotional outbursts and became the voice of reason if and when I needed one.

We talked about everything. The medical progress on your diagnosis, my legal team, and the sequence of events that unfolded as a result of my desire to keep you out of state custody. She never pushed too far, only asking about what she knew I would tell her, but her questions often made me think.

I went to see her after my conference call with the lawyers. I was mentally preparing myself for the realization that I might have to pack up my house and move my family somewhere unfamiliar. The intended parents had not made any real indication of wanting to be a part of the decision. Sharon's final clarification email kept playing over and over in my mind:

> The Intended Parents did not file for the Parental Order, so they will not be considered the legal parents of the child, should the child be born. You will be the only person who will be making decisions about the child, should the child be born.

And in an email from Roger and Ursula's lawyer, I had no doubt I was on my own:

> On February 16, Ms. Kelley initially refused to comply with the terms of the Agreement after receiving the sonographic results at Hartford Hospital. In my letter on February 22, Ms. Kelley was given further notice of her ongoing breach. Her ten-day period to cure has expired. Ms. Kelley is in breach, thereby relieving my clients of any further obligation under the Agreement.

I sat on an oversized leather couch in Christina's office,

staring at her perfect ivory skin. Glancing around at her meticulously organized work space, I wondered if her house looked as magazine-ready as this room.

"I want to help her," I said, tapping my fingers on the arm of the couch. "I don't want to bring her into the world and then dump her off, never to see or hear about her again. It isn't right."

"Just remember," Christina said, "you didn't ask for this. You wanted to help people create life. How were you to know anything about the shadowy, dark side of surrogacy that nobody talks about?" She paused, looking thoughtfully at me. "Now you've been put in a bad position and you're doing the best you can. But you can't leave your values and feelings by the wayside. Your opinions have value, like the life of that child has value to you. That will never change. It's not surprising that you feel as though you are responsible for her, even though that wasn't the case when all this started."

"I just wish things could have gone differently."

"There's a level of responsibility that comes with making choices such as these. You have to assume the role of sole provider in the reality of the legal system, and that makes this experience something that weighs heavily on you. Whether or not you choose to parent her, you are always going to have a connection with her. You are sacrificing a lot to give her a chance."

Christina's words were simple, yet poignant. As she had many times before, she put my own thoughts into one cohesive breath, thus validating my point of view and giving me confidence to make tough decisions.

We talked for another fifteen minutes until it was time for Christina to see another patient.

"Thanks for your advice today," I said, standing up to give her a hug.

"Anytime. I do hope this all works out in the end. We'll talk again," she said, leading me to the door.

As I walked out of her office, I knew the decision of whether to stay or leave had been made. I could not question that anymore. The logistics of where to go, however, was much more tedious. There would be a lot of work ahead, no matter what location I decided on. Just as I had when I was faced with the demand to abort, I called the person who knew me best.

"I talked with Michael and an adoption lawyer in Michigan today, Mom. They think it will work out very well. Michigan has declared surrogacy agreements inadmissible in court and they have one of the best hospitals in the country."

"Sounds great! Did you ask about Missouri?"

"Well, the hospital isn't as good and there aren't any surrogacy laws. I really want to be near you, though. I could stay at your place in Illinois and Bethany could help with the girls. That way you'd be close by."

"It's a hard decision, I know. Whatever you decide, it's going to be fine."

"I don't know about that, Mom. How am I supposed to live in a state where nothing is familiar and where I know no one? Nobody! I don't have any money. I can't get a job now. I feel like it's never going to work. Michigan is great but I have nothing set up." I began to cry.

Then she muttered the words that changed everything. "You tell me where you're going and we'll make it happen."

I sat in my car, unable to speak at first, my head resting on the back of my seat. "What do you mean?"

"I mean you figure out where it is going to be best for you to have that baby and I will help you to make it happen."

CHAPTER TWENTY

"Umm... okay." Still in disbelief I tried to gather my thoughts.

"It sounds like Michigan is going to be the best choice. Am I right?"

"Yeah, Mom. You are. I really want to come out to Missouri, though. I don't know. Maybe I should wait till tomorrow and talk to the Missouri attorney that Michael contacted."

"Crystal, think about this. You've made the hard decision, and no matter what, you have the backing to go wherever this baby needs to go to be born."

"Okay," I said, my mind made up. "Michigan it is."

"When do we leave?"

> No one else will ever know the strength of my love for you. After all, you're the only one who knows what my heart sounds like from the inside.
>
> —Unknown

CHAPTER TWENTY-ONE
March 29, 2012

"**A**re you sure you have everything you need?"

"Yes, Dad."

"You have water? Change for the tolls? Snacks? Your directions?"

"I have a GPS, Dad. Two of them in fact. And my cell phone charger. I'll be okay."

"All right, I'm just checking. You know I have to. I'm your father."

"Yeah, Dad. I know."

"And you're meeting your mom when?"

"In a little over twenty-four hours. Dad, I've got to go."

"All right... I love you. Drive carefully and call me when you get there."

"I will, Dad. I love you too."

I shook my head as I hung up the phone. My father had called at least three times since I left the house. He thought of little things like telling me not to forget to change my oil and to stop in Pennsylvania to get gas because it was cheaper than filling up in New York.

I had never been to Michigan before, Stormie, and hoped I could secure our living situation and your care in the few days I would have there before we officially called it home. Michael had warned me to be vigilant until I was actually able to leave. Although the intended parents had not made any legal contact in the last few weeks, there was no way of knowing exactly what they were planning. We all believed that it would be detrimental for you to be born in a state with such limited resources for your care, so the implications of being served with a summons would have halted every plan I had. I could have been forced to stay in Connecticut, where I would lose you to the system, standing helplessly by with no authority for your well-being. I would have no possible way to influence decisions made by the state for your care, and who knew how well that would turn out.

My decision to go to Michigan was the first step in what I believed to be the freedom to give you the best I possibly could. At the time I still wasn't quite sure what that meant, but I would work as hard as I could so that you would be well taken care of.

I sat in my seat with my pillow in the small of my back for support, and pushed the 'Go' button on the Garmin. As I pulled out of the gas station and onto the highway I felt both excited and nervous at the same time. There was a lot of work to be done.

I used my time while driving as wisely as I could. I was in

contact with the University of Michigan's pediatric hospital, and had started the preliminary work towards getting an appointment. I had searched online and found some prospective housing solutions, and had reservations to look at three separate apartments being sublet by U of M students who were not staying for the summer. I had people to call regarding caring for my dog, who would not be able to come to Michigan with us, and others to reach concerning resources I had found through social media. I had a lot of phone calls to make and was grateful for the wireless headset I had picked up with the few dollars I had left over after purchasing some essentials for my trip. I would make the trek alone, sans Emmy and Anne, who were spending the weekend with their grandparents.

Leaving Connecticut also meant I didn't have to be worried about being served while I was there. I would spend a few days in Michigan then return to Connecticut, staying at my house for another week or so, then with a friend in between leases.

I was really nervous about finding an apartment that was cheap enough as well as big enough and safe for my kids. Ann Arbor is a college town, and most of the apartments I was looking at were sublets of students' apartments. Who knew what kind of an environment I would be putting myself and my family into?

■　■　■

The ride to Michigan was long. I left early in the morning and arrived at the home of one of my social media contacts around 1 a.m. I was exhausted, and at nearly seven months pregnant it took quite a toll on my body.

I had never before met my online friend in person and was very grateful for the invitation to stay with her, breaking up the hundreds of miles I had to travel alone. My host was very accommodating. Her baby was a patient at the hospital where I would deliver and she understood the pressure I had felt from the doctors to abort.

She invited me in, grabbing my luggage from me as I walked up to her front porch.

"How was your trip so far?" she asked. The small picture I had seen of her on Facebook did not do her beauty any justice. Although her baggy pajamas and messy hair made her look every bit the tired mom, her bright smile and helpful nature radiated a feeling of warm friendship.

"So far, so good," I replied, following her inside. "Thank you again for taking me in."

"Of course, Crystal. There was no way you could endure that trip the entire way without stopping." She led me to my room upstairs. "Here's where you can sleep tonight."

The room was painted a pale green with matching yellow and green striped curtains. "This is perfect. Thank you."

"I'll let you settle in. Do you want to have some tea or are you ready for bed?"

"I'd actually like to stay up for a bit and chat if you don't mind. I should be tired but I haven't been out of the car all day and my mind is still in high gear."

"I'm still wide awake so I'll meet you downstairs in the living room when you're ready."

I left my bags on the floor and went to find the bathroom to freshen up. I crept down the hall, careful not to wake her children.

The bathroom was small, but all I needed was a splash of water on my face to make me feel refreshed.

I dried my face with a towel draped over the sink and

headed downstairs where I found my new friend sitting on the couch, waiting for me.

"Come. Sit down. You have to be tired," she said, patting the seat next to her.

"More mentally exhausted than anything."

We began the conversation talking about the doctors we had encountered as mothers and how so many looked at disabled children as imperfect.

"You'd be surprised how many of them claim that they want to treat babies with specific problems when really they are convincing more than half of those parents to abort their babies," she said.

The statement resonated with what I had heard previously through the heart and adoption groups. Babies with disabilities were being aborted without so much as a chance at life and the doctors were the ones telling the parents to do it. I remembered how I had felt during the initial ultrasound when the doctor explained that 'the fetus' would have a sub-par life, and the insinuation of the agent during our meeting that disabled babies were a burden upon families.

As we were talking about how we could change the way families brought their special-needs babies into the world, I felt myself starting to fall asleep on the couch. My host went to make us a pot of coffee but I drifted off into a deep slumber.

Loud piercing bells ringing and dinging from my phone woke me the next morning. My mother had arranged to meet me at the Detroit airport and here I was, still three hours away. I ran up the stairs to the bedroom where my luggage was and peeked into my host's room.

"I'm late. I have to go. Thanks again," I whispered.

"Oh, 'bye, Crystal," she said, springing up from her pillow. "Please let me know if you ever need anything. It was so nice to meet you in person."

"You too," I said, closing her door and hobbling down the steps with my bags to the front door.

I spent the first hour of my ride fighting the urge to pull over and go back to sleep in my backseat. I called my mother a few minutes before I found the exit for the airport and by 10 a.m. the runways of the busy terminals came into view. She said she would be waiting for me at the passenger pickup point, red umbrella in hand. I was excited to see her but a bit anxious about the tasks we were about to embark on.

I pulled up to the pickup area, easily spotting the red umbrella and my mother's tall stance.

"Hi, Mom," I yelled out the window.

"What's our first order of business?" she asked, throwing her large duffle bag into my backseat.

"The University of Michigan."

We had to get to know the area and the best way to do that was to see it for ourselves.

Surrounded by bright green grass, the massive stone buildings of the University rose from the landscape like ancient stately castles. Students carrying stacks of books with backpacks hanging off one shoulder walked arm-in-arm down the elegant sidewalks of the campus. We drove around the University and then through the busy streets of Ann Arbor, on our way to meet one of my internet contacts at a local restaurant.

My connection to the doula groups online had given me a great resource, a doula by the name of Stacy Thompson. As an experienced mom and doula, Stacy knew I was going to need a tremendous amount of assistance while I got acclimated to the area. She told me she felt drawn to help me bring you into the world and offered her personal pool of resources.

The restaurant was quaint, with students drinking their coffee and studying for their next big examination. When we arrived Stacy was already seated at a booth, her hair a golden blonde, falling just below her shoulders. We chatted mostly about you, Stormie. She already had volunteers lined up to help me before, during, and after your birth and assured me my time in Michigan would be worth it. We talked for about forty minutes then Stacy had to leave to relieve her babysitter.

After our conversation with my new friend I felt even more strongly that Michigan was a fantastic choice for you. Her kind words and supportive nature came during my most vulnerable hours and I could not thank her enough for her help. My mother seemed pleased, and we both voiced how impressed we were with Stacy's preparation.

An hour later, exhaustion had once again set in. To ensure that there would not be too much we would have to do during our together-time, I was pleased that I had made a large portion of the preliminary phone calls and appointments during my drive to Michigan. After driving around town for hours and meeting with Stacy, it was time for a nap.

We arrived at the bed and breakfast where we would be spending the weekend. It was a beautiful Victorian home, complete with intricate cornices and a large turret extending into the sky above. We unloaded our bags and walked towards the elegant, frosted french doors that signified the entrance. Wearing a flowered dress and small silver glasses that sat on the bridge of her nose, the little old woman who ran the inn greeted us. She commented immediately on the size of my stomach.

"Oh, Honey, aren't you adorable. You have to be pretty far along. What are you doing traveling at this time?"

Her comment on my seemingly enormous belly both irritated and amused me. If this little woman knew what was going on with our lives at the time and the real reason behind my excursion to Michigan, she would certainly understand why my travel plans were necessary.

I smiled, my fake little sarcastic smile where one corner of my mouth rose higher than the other, and carefully dragged my suitcase up the winding staircase to our room. There were two small beds with a little hideaway cubby that had a sink and a bathroom. A small bookcase in the corner housed a coffee pot and microwave. Hot cocoa mix, mugs, a large bowl, and some popcorn accompanied the appliances, together with a sign urging us to pick out a movie from the bookcase on the stairwell. 'Hope Floats' caught my eye and we attempted to watch it, but were so exhausted from the day of traveling that we fell asleep long before the end credits rolled.

■ ■ ■

The next two days felt like five. We had so much to do and only two days in which to do it. We visited the Department of Health, Woman, Infants and Children; a bank; and one apartment in just the first day.

The apartment we had looked at was perfect for our needs. It was a fairly large two-bedroom with a big living room and small kitchen. The kitchen had an eat-in area at the end of the room next to the portable dishwasher. It was definitely cramped, but it was nothing less than what I needed.

"You know I won't be cooking any more than absolutely necessary, right, Mom?"

She laughed. "That place would work out pretty well," she said. "But there's nowhere really for the kids to play. Let's see what we find tomorrow and we'll go from there."

By the time we got back to the bed and breakfast, we were both completely drained, but we couldn't sleep. You were pretty active too, Stormie. We stayed up late, catching up on life, chatting about you and the girls, and discussing what we had left to do to keep the momentum going. I was considering staying in Michigan after your birth since I had been thinking of getting out of Connecticut altogether for a while. Maybe this was just the push I needed. As we finally started to wind down from the busy day, I commented that everything seemed to be falling into place. Then my mother asked the question I had been dreading since I picked her up at the airport.

"So what are you going to do after she's born?"

I shook my head and sighed. I didn't really have an answer. In the last few weeks I had explored every avenue and had every opinion possible thrown at me from multiple angles. Every one of them had positives and negatives. Adoption sounded like the best option, but I was very hesitant about allowing someone else to care for you in the way I thought was most beneficial.

"I don't know, Mom. I don't feel like I can count on anybody to love her and make the best decisions for her. I mean, her own biological parents gave up on her with barely a second thought. The girls are starting to call her 'our baby' and 'Stormie.' I don't know if I want to let someone else raise her. I mean, really, since that ultrasound I have been the only one fighting for her. Who can say that someone else isn't going to give up on her just like they did?"

CHAPTER TWENTY-ONE

"You know, Crystal, you can love her without keeping her. But I understand where the feelings come from. You basically got thrown into being this child's primary salvation without the consideration of how it would affect you. They haven't made it easy. Of course you feel like the only one fighting. After all, you are still fighting."

She rolled over in her bed, staring at the ceiling. "Think about it," she said. "Like everything else, either it will fall into place or it won't."

I couldn't stop thinking about those words. I had dreams of people coming to take you away from me, punching them with my fists flying yet striking air. I woke up in the middle of the night to a flurry of activity in my belly. You were very agitated, Stormie. I got up to use the bathroom but that didn't settle you like it usually did. As I sat on the bed in the dimly lit room I thought about the reality of the situation I was facing as you got closer to being born.

No one knew what was actually going to happen once you were born. The social worker at U of M hospital had told me not to be too sure of what the cardiologists there would say.

"Opinions change depending on which hospital you are talking to and the ability of their staff," she had said.

As happy as I was that the University of Michigan thought they could handle my case, I was also still very anxious about how drastically my life was going to change if I went to Michigan. Having lost all my income I was having a hard time figuring out how I was going to support myself and the girls while we were there. My mother would help, but it wasn't fair for me to depend on her. I would be on my own, with a child who would possibly need very long and complicated hospitalization. Medicaid would pay for some of it, but they didn't have a reputation for paying for things blindly.

In the quiet of the night my mind wandered, keeping me up long into the early hours of the morning. It was then, Stormie, that I felt what I can only describe as a moment of clarity. The answer was easy—I had to give you up for adoption. It wouldn't be fair to my little girls to keep you and it wouldn't be the right thing for you either. There were families who had already contacted me, telling me they would love to adopt you, but due to my hesitance I hadn't responded to any of them. Still, they were there. These families could without a second thought financially support the type of care you were probably going to need—families who cared about your welfare and would be happy to offer you a home.

At that moment I realized I had options. Of course, I had no idea how I would make that ultimate decision, but I knew it had to be something I pursued a little more seriously.

■　■　■

When morning came, Mom and I dragged ourselves out of bed.

"Sleep well?" she asked.

"Well enough," I replied, stroking my belly. "Had some good thinking time at 2 a.m. when this little miss decided it was playtime."

"Oh good."

We looked at another apartment that day, on the other side of the U of M campus. This place was much smaller, and the rooms were at opposite ends of the apartment. I was concerned about that, given how much Anne liked raiding the refrigerator in the middle of the night. But we put in an application anyway.

CHAPTER TWENTY-ONE

The second appointment of the day was cancelled so we were left to explore the town again for the afternoon. When we met at the airport it had seemed like an insurmountable task had been placed before us, but on that second day there was very little left undone. We puttered around town and discovered another adorable quaint little town about fifteen minutes away. Ypsilanti served as our oasis for the rest of our time in Michigan. This adorable little diner on the main strip had the best fried macaroni and cheese I had ever tasted. The attached store sold all-natural wholesome snacks and we got some of their chocolate-covered pretzels for later.

"So what do you think?" my mother asked.

"The first apartment is perfect. It's also a little more expensive."

"I think you offer the people with the apartment you love a little less money than their asking price and get a better apartment, Crystal. You have to live within your means, and your means are very slim."

I knew what she meant. Child support and help from others was all I had to rely on for money to support all of us.

A few moments later my phone rang. It was the people with the apartment that I really wanted. "We'd like you to take it," they told me.

I put my mother on the phone. "Include the electric in the price and you've got a deal."

There was some chatter in a foreign language in the background, and then silence.

"All right, we'll do that."

A smile crossed my mother's face as she nodded her head and gave me a thumbs-up.

It was mine, Stormie, it was mine.

Next morning after she took her bags out of the trunk of my
car at the airport she hugged me tightly. "You're doing a great thing,
Crystal. Be proud of that, even if it is hard right now. One day you'll
come out on the other side and it'll all have been worth it."

"Yeah, but what about Stormie? What does she have to look
forward to?"

She paused for a minute, deep in thought. "I can't answer
that for you. You care about her, and rightfully so, but you have
some very complicated things to work through in order to find an
answer. In the end, though, I think you'll do what's right. Not for
you necessarily, but for her."

After waving goodbye to my mom, I began the long ride
home. Over seven hundred miles of driving left me with hour
upon hour to think about your future. As I drove, I thought about
the pursuit of adoption and my intention to send you to a family
that not only wanted you, but had the means to best treat whatever
challenges you might have.

I had received adoption offers since the very beginning, but I
didn't consider many of them to be genuinely interested as they had
not kept in contact or asked about your progress. A family member,
though removed, had made an offer of adoption as well. Yet none
of the offers presented seemed like the right ones to choose. Most
of them were strangers, so what type of relationship would they
be willing to have with me? How would building that relationship
work?

However, I had left them all in my email inbox, just in case.

At a rest stop I pulled up my Facebook account and emails
on my phone. One person stood out, but she was still mostly
unfamiliar, and then there was someone else further down the
coast. They were both pretty active on my page. One was a fellow

CHAPTER TWENTY-ONE

doula in Virginia and the other had created a heart support group in a different state, and served as a great congenital heart defect resource. I'd had multiple, extensive conversations about your condition and developments in your prognosis with each of them for varying reasons and had become pretty close with both.

■   ■   ■

I finally reached Pennsylvania and marveled at the serenity of the view. From the highway the mountains were breathtaking and I pulled the car over to a scenic overlook. The stillness of the landscape before me and the peace, beauty, and perfection was like the sign I had been waiting for. Things had gone so well in Michigan and I intuitively felt as though adoption was destined. I had always been a big believer in karma, fate, and the imperfect perfection of nature. The scene on that mountaintop as the sun started to set made me realize that my answer had been right in front of me the entire time. How can anyone say there is no rhyme or reason to the creation of life? Perhaps the answer is that the beauty of life does not come from the individual shape of each creation, but from the beauty they create when they are all together as a whole. As individuals, we are all flawed. But when we stand together we make something exquisite.

As I drove down the mountain I felt the last rays of the sun through the window, filling me with warmth and relaxing my soul. I had made up my mind.

When I arrived home, I made a quick call to Michael who confirmed that nothing had happened on the legal front while I had been gone. Without Emmy or Anne home yet, it presented the perfect opportunity to call the family I had chosen and ask them to come up and meet me. I had spoken to Rachel a few times recently and was convinced I was making the right choice.

"Rachel. It's been decided. I'm going to Michigan."

"Oh my goodness. Well I'm glad you made a decision. They have a great hospital."

"There's something else."

"What is it?"

I found it hard to force the words out of my lips. "I... you... remember what you said way back when we first talked. About adoption?"

"Yes."

"Well, I've decided that I really need to seriously look at it as an option. And I'd like you to be the ones that take her home."

"Oh. My. Wow, Crystal! I don't know what to say. Of course we will."

And so I decided, Stormie. And then I wavered, and then I decided again. I changed my mind a thousand times a day and said I was going to keep you, but something always made me want you to be a part of a family I knew could financially support all your needs.

Three days before I was scheduled to leave, Rachel and her husband, and Scott and my father all came over and we spent the day packing boxes and moving furniture. The moment I laid eyes on Rachel I knew she would be the perfect mother for you. She immediately hugged me as I opened my front door to let them in, her delicate hands moving gently up and down my back.

"We're so glad you chose us," she said.

Her husband was equally as genuine, shaking my father's hand and telling Scott I had made the best decision for you. They expressed their desire to give you everything they could and I believed every word.

We moved my entire apartment into storage that day, resting sporadically throughout the afternoon to take a swig of water, getting to know one another as we loaded everything into our vehicles.

As the day ended we agreed to keep in touch. I promised I would update them on your condition as soon as I was able.

APRIL 8, 2012

The days were counting down, but there were still a few things I needed to do. I wasn't sure how long it would take to get my first appointment in Michigan, so I decided to go for the next ultrasound appointment I had scheduled with one of the practices where I had been receiving follow-up care. I didn't expect much, except that I wanted to make sure you were still growing on your own personal five to ten percent curve.

You were sleeping when I arrived at the doctor's practice and I was thankful for that because it meant I could pay closer attention while the technician did his measurements. In the middle of breaking up the third fight between Emmy and Anne, the geneticist came in and spoke with the technician. She brought me to a different room, shut the door, and proceeded to use what I considered far too vulgar language in front of a two and three-year-old.

"This baby... she won't live very far past birth, if she even survives."

I stared blankly at her. I was leaving town in a couple of days to try to give you a chance at life. What did she mean by 'if she even survives?'

"Her hands. They don't open. It's a marker for neurological defects. Your baby already has heart defects and it looks like she's going to have neurological ones as well. These babies are often born not breathing or able to swallow."

"Well, I know swallowing isn't a problem. She's got hiccups all the time."

She looked at me, rolling her eyes. "That doesn't mean anything."

I stuttered and stammered. "Well, it doesn't change anything at this point. She's coming."

I left that appointment in a state of shock, escaping without Anne's Care Bear figures we had left on the geneticist's desk. Every step I took away from the practice, I repeated, "You'll prove them wrong, Stormie. You'll prove them wrong." It was like a chant, a mantra to keep you safe, growing, and as close to okay as I could hope you would be. I got into my car and quickly decided to make one more stop. I had to be ready.

I left Emmy and Anne with their grandparents and made my way across town. I held back tears as I drove, arriving a few minutes later in the parking lot of the grand building.

I walked up to the oversized gold front doors, my hands shaking as I grabbed the handle. A man and woman in tailored black suits held the doors open for me. I knew this place well. My grandfather had been brought here, and I had seen several friends pass through as well.

They led me to a conference room and I sat at a long table, perusing through booklets on different types of ceremonies and tributes one could purchase to celebrate the life and store the mementoes of death of a dear loved one. I glanced through pictures of mahogany coffins and white dove releases, but nothing referred to what to do when a child passes. My heart grew heavy in my chest and tears welled in my eyes as I imagined the pain of possibly burying you. It was something I hoped I would never have to experience. However, if something were to happen to you, I wanted to be prepared.

I asked question after question, listening intently to their responses, and when it was over I left as quickly as I possibly could. They told me they would prepare for the worst, and I had seen enough to know that if you died I would probably not recover for a very long time. So much of myself was, and still is, invested in your life, Stormie. I wanted to celebrate life with you and it terrified me that I might not ever get that chance.

It is not
the mountain
we conquer
but ourselves.

—Sophocles

CHAPTER TWENTY-TWO
April 10, 2012

It was a warm seventy-eight degrees in Ann Arbor, Michigan according to my not-so-smart phone. I made sure I packed short sleeve shirts and sandals for Emmy and Anne, and bought you the cutest spring outfit for your arrival. It was the last item I had yet to pack in your bag. I held it up in front of me and smiled at the embroidered flowers adorning the chest of the onesie and the cute, pink and white striped pants that matched. I couldn't wait to finally meet you and see what you looked like filling out this lovely outfit.

I had left my apartment days ago, and we stayed with Scott until it was time to leave. Our last few days in Connecticut were full of visitors saying goodbye and trips to see people who I needed or wanted to say goodbye to before I left.

With our final hours together we spent a good part of the day running around and the last half enjoying our time with Scott. It was going to be a while until the girls saw their father again, and even though I wasn't thrilled with how things were currently between us, I didn't want to take the time with their father away from them. I napped while the girls and Scott read books, watched movies, and made dinner together. It was sweet to see him being a dad again.

"I still can't believe you're driving to Michigan by yourself with your two daughters. Isn't it like twelve hours away?" Lisette asked when she came to say her final goodbyes.

"Something like that. I'm not expecting to make it all the way there without stopping. We'll have to stay somewhere overnight."

"Do you have enough money for that?"

"I have somewhere to go. Plus I've saved some and also got donations from a website I set up," I replied, folding the onesie and striped pants into your bulging suitcase of clothes. "We'll be okay."

I zipped up your bag and slung the strap over my shoulder, then bent down to get Anne and Emmy's bags.

"Meet you outside," Lisette said, lugging a few blankets and the duffle bag to the front door.

I followed close behind and we piled almost everything we had into the back of the Camry.

Anne turned round in her car seat to face me as I passed her open window. "Are we leaving now?" she asked, her eyes half closed having just woken up from a short nap.

"Soon," I replied.

Scott closed the trunk and gave me a big hug. "You be careful," he said. "And please call me when you get there. I need to know you're safe."

"I will. I promise."

"Crystal. I hope you know I believe in what you're doing," Scott said.

Turning my head to hide my misted-up eyes, I pulled away from his strong embrace and got into the driver's seat.

Before I closed the door, I looked up at Lisette who was staring down at me with tears in her eyes. "It's not like I'm leaving forever," I said.

"I know," she stuttered. "I know."

I closed the door and stared blankly at the steering wheel, tears beginning to fall from my eyes as well.

I may not have ever truly loved living in Connecticut, but it was home. I waved to Scott and Lisette who were standing on the porch of the condo, and told the girls to wave goodbye as we pulled out towards the street for the long journey ahead. Emmy whimpered a little and Anne started to cry. I dug into one of the bags behind my chair for a book to occupy the girls. The bag of books was easy to find, but the book I wanted was stuck. I yanked and pulled, pushing toys, clothes and baby gear out of the way, finally releasing it. I handed it to Anne.

Getting on the highway I had a sudden wave of what I can only describe as relief. It was weird, Stormie. I had dreamed of leaving Connecticut for so long, but I would never have guessed that this was how it was going to happen.

The Constitution state didn't exactly provide the necessary resources I needed to make sure you had the best life possible. If I stayed, I would have to turn you over to the state and I could not imagine a worse fate, other than the one your intended parents had wanted. In Michigan I would be recognized as your mother and could therefore make the best decision I could for your care. I felt it was my only option to ensure your birth and a family who would care for you like their own. And so I drove.

■　■　■

It was just over six hours since I left Connecticut when my gas indicator lit up my dashboard. I pulled into a rest stop off highway 80, just before Dubois, Pennsylvania. Anne had fallen asleep but Emmy was wide awake, squealing and laughing at the stuffed animal elephant Lisette had given her before we left.

I wasn't used to paying under three dollars a gallon for gas but I welcomed the cost in Pennsylvania since every single cent spent meant less to live on while we were in Michigan.

I had not talked to Roger and Ursula since the day at the geneticist's office when they told me they wanted to abort you. As Catholics, their decision shocked me. They were rightfully devastated with your diagnosis but I never thought they would only want a *perfect* you. And even though I wasn't sure anyone else would be your best option for a mother after you were born, Scott helped me realize that we couldn't financially care for you the way you needed to be cared for. However, I would do the one thing I could and if that meant leaving Connecticut for Michigan, then that was the path I would take.

The hours crept on, and the warm spring air filled the car. I had thought of everything, my CD book on my passenger seat and a box full of snacks on the floor. I was prepared for anything. I listened to the radio for as long as I could pick up my favorite stations and then I switched to CDs. I had a destination and enough food and gas to get where I needed to go.

I looked in my rearview mirror to check on Anne and Emmy who were fast asleep, their heads tilted awkwardly in their car seats. I turned my gaze towards the road, blinking several times to keep myself awake.

Pulling into the driveway of a Facebook friend who had offered me shelter, I was relieved to see that the lights were still on in her house. I could see her peeking through the front window, waving as she saw me get out of my car.

I brought Anne and Emmy in one by one and carried them up to the room where we would stay. Neither woke up as I pulled back the covers and tucked them in.

"I can't thank you enough for letting us stay here," I said to my friend as I made my way down the stairs.

"Of course. I couldn't imagine doing what you have taken on." she said.

We spent over an hour talking about you, Stormie, and about her daughter's journey, before my eyes would no longer remain open.

"I'm sorry. I have to go to sleep. We still have a long drive tomorrow," I said, giving her a hug.

"I completely understand. See you in the morning," she said.

In another room upstairs there was a long sectional couch that had a comfortable chaise on one end. I curled up with the blankets that were set out for me and quickly fell asleep.

Just six hours later, I opened my eyes to Emmy climbing in next to me. I was too big, and the couch too small, to make either of us comfortable, so I covered Emmy up with the blanket and went downstairs to grab something to eat.

No one else in the house was up. We were four hours away from our destination and since I was already up I decided to wake the girls, get a head start on our journey and arrive there sooner than expected.

Emmy was still curled into a ball on the couch in the room I had slept in, so I crept past her and into Anne's room, pulling back the covers and cradling her in my arms. She stayed asleep while I buckled her into her car seat. I went back inside and knelt down next to Emmy. "Honey, we have to go," I said, gently shaking her to try to rouse her from sleep. "Honey, time to get up." Her eyes fluttered open to tiny slits, quickly closing again as I carried her like a baby down the stairs and into the car. I ran back into the house one last time, grabbed some muffins my friend had set out for breakfast for the road and left a note on the kitchen table, thanking my gracious host for offering her home to me a second time.

In just under four hours, we arrived at the brick building that was to be our new home; an apartment in a college town was not exactly what the girls and I were used to, but it would do for the few months we needed to stay.

As we pulled up, a petite dark-haired woman jumped out of a blue Civic and ran over. She surprised me but then I realized that I had almost forgotten that Stacy had arranged for some of her friends to be there to help me get things from my car into the apartment. Tears filled my eyes. I had expected to carry all the boxes in myself.

Her friend Toni and her husband lifted the TV out first and set it up quickly in the living room. The apartment was rented furnished, so I had two couches, tables and beds already in place. As we brought all the stuff inside, the girls sat on the couch and watched a movie with a bag of Pirate's Booty Snack Mix. It was still early when we brought the last few boxes in. It wasn't much, but it was enough. The girls and I would sleep in one room, with the other bedroom serving as a playroom. The kitchen was like an office for me—a television sitting in one corner with a computer system and my sewing machines in another. Stacy and Toni had arranged for a few other people to stop by, bringing items I had forgotten to take with me like dish detergent and garbage bags.

We spent most of the day setting up the house, but by about two o'clock I was tired. Emmy still napped regularly, so I headed to the bedroom to try to get her to sleep while the visitors gathered their tools and let themselves out. I fell asleep soon after Emmy, leaving Anne playing in the adjoining room with the toys we had brought with us. When we woke up I made some macaroni and cheese then decided it was time to show the girls the area. We were all still tired, but I had a little money in my pocket left over from the trip, and I knew of a great smoothie place.

We walked down the street and around the corner. As soon as Anne saw the striped red umbrella over a picnic table on the sidewalk she gasped and started jumping up and down. When we stepped into the tiny little trailer and ordered our drinks, I knelt down so I was at eye level with both the children and held their hands.

"This town is where we live now, okay? We have to work together and help each other get through the next couple of months until the baby comes. You guys are going to do great, right?"

Their enthusiastic nods made me smile. I knew it was an act that wouldn't last long, but they were so cute in their desperate attempt to get their hands on a smoothie. We passed around hugs and then went to sit outside.

■　■　■

That night I put the girls to bed a little earlier than normal. Eight o'clock seemed like midnight and I was tired and sore from driving, unpacking, and then walking to the smoothie place. The apartment seemed bare, and I could see the light from out in the hallway and heard the door slam every time someone came through. It was hard to adjust to, Stormie, but it was our temporary home until you were born. I lay down, putting my head on my pillow next to Emmy's tiny body, and gently rubbed my belly.

"It'll all be okay, Stormie," I said. "We're in the best place for you. You'll be fine."

I thought that if I said those words out loud it would give us a greater chance to hear your first cry and that you would defy what the doctors were saying and take your first breath. I stared at the ceiling, clenching my jaw as I thought about what our future together would be like. I hoped the relationship between me and your adoptive parents would build into a strong friendship over time and that their promise to keep me in your life would be fulfilled. I couldn't imagine handing you over to them and never seeing you again. I had carried you for nine months, and while I had never expected to become so attached to you, our bond now could not be broken.

> To conquer
> fear is the
> beginning
> of wisdom.
>
> —Bertrand Russell

CHAPTER TWENTY-THREE
April, 2012

We spent the next few days exploring our new town, walking down the sidewalks lined with bookstores, restaurants, and little mom and pop shops. I had gained such a small amount of weight that from the back you still couldn't tell I was pregnant. From the front, though, I was huge, and with my belly constantly in the way the stroller I had for Emmy soon became awkward to push. I often had Anne push her so that I didn't have to lean over and strain my back.

In the evening hours the campus area was busy; the restaurant patios were bustling with patrons, and the streets were lined with cars. But on the outskirts of the campus the atmosphere was different; a sense of peace pervaded the scenery, with beautiful houses and well-manicured lawns, mostly student housing, but without the frenzied business of the campus area. I enjoyed walking in both areas, although the girls certainly liked the quieter neighborhoods better because I let them run ahead on the sidewalks.

During the day people gathered for group activities like Frisbee, or used the green as a shortcut across campus, but as the sun began to set there were less people in sight. The large grassy areas served as the perfect spot to let the girls run around for a little while.

■ ■ ■

As Emmy, Anne and I walked around the campus every day and students lugging heavy backpacks hurried to their summer classes, curious eyes stared back at me, forcing me to look away. The stark contrast of my pregnant body and the two children constantly toddling behind me did make me different from the others in town. While gazes followed, with the occasional hushed remark or two wondering who I was and why I was alone, I knew my thoughts were not rational and that the people I saw on the street would have had no idea how I had come to live in Michigan, so I could not blame them for noticing me. After all, a college campus was not a place you expected to see a pregnant mother with two children.

My differences were less prominent when I ventured off campus to go grocery shopping or visit nearby towns. There were many people who offered small gestures of kindness when they saw me with my two young daughters. Some would help put my groceries into the car; others held the door for me as we walked into a store, Anne holding my hand and Emmy on my hip.

The apartment where we lived was a typical college apartment house. None of the people who lived there had children; most were students at the University of Michigan who kept to themselves. I met a few of my neighbors at various times, usually when I was struggling with Emmy in the stroller or venturing to the front lobby to get the mail. I was grateful for their pleasantries and recalled myself at that age, thinking I knew everything. They didn't have to be kind to me but most of them were.

That did not hold true for everyone, though. There was one apartment on my level full of college boys—loud, arrogant, and foreign. Since my apartment was tucked in the corner of the building I could hear much of what went on in the hallways and stairwells. The security door reverberated through the entire apartment, especially at night, slamming as partygoers came and went. I only saw the foreigners in passing, consistently making derogatory comments about me and my kids as they walked past my apartment. A few times I thought about calling the campus police as their screams penetrated the walls into the early morning hours while Emmy and Anne were trying to sleep. I often found liquor bottles scattered near my front door, beer dripping out of the tops creating small pools on the floor.

For the most part, though, our time in Ann Arbor was very pleasant. Stacy Thompson had given me phone numbers for a few doulas in the area and many of them would stop by, occasionally taking us out to eat or to fun activities for the girls. Some were not available for your birth but were more than willing to help out with whatever we needed. Anne and Emmy had a lot of fun playing with their kids and our friendships enabled us to explore some of the neighboring towns together.

In the first few weeks we were in town, both my girls came

down with Chickenpox. It certainly wasn't ideal to keep them quarantined from the rest of society until they healed, but it gave the three of us quality time to spend together. As they got progressively better each day, we finished hanging photos on the walls and watched movies. When we passed the two week incubation period we resumed our daily walks around campus, continuing to receive stares since Anne and Emmy's faces were covered in tiny pink dots.

Living on campus I definitely got my required exercise. I refused to drive my car unless I was going to the grocery store or somewhere further away, so we walked almost everywhere. We didn't have much money, or memberships to any activity centers, and there was only one playground within walking distance. We would have picnics on the grass and watch the birds fly overhead and take pieces of bread we tossed to them. Every day our path was different. There were times when we took three walks a day—my desperate attempt at releasing the pent up energy of two young children with nowhere to run and jump.

I tried to join a few moms' groups but never really participated with any of the mothers. I wanted Anne and Emmy to make some friends but I became closed off, afraid of the unforseen consequences of telling anyone who I was. While the children played, many of the mothers would gather in small groups, discussing their husbands and the rooms they were redoing in their posh houses. I never felt like my experiences were relevant. I tried several different groups, even one for adoptive families that was willing to accept me, but nothing ever seemed to click.

Attempting to make new friends had only isolated me even further and I decided to simply go about my days doing what I could just to get you to your birth. The hospital staff and doulas became my friends; they were the only people I could count on and

who understood my situation. They made my time there much more
pleasant.

Even with my antisocial tendencies, with all the artsy activities offered in Ann Arbor, and the three or four people I met who took us on little adventures, we quickly filled up our summer schedule. The area was gorgeous at that time of year.

Every three to four days someone would show up and we'd plan a fun day, touring the local museums, art shows, and doula networking events. It was freeing to be away from the pressure of the Stones' control, and I was more than happy to allow Herb to address the legal issues.

■　■　■

The doctors in Michigan wanted to do all their own testing to see what challenges you had as you developed, so this kept me busy, Stormie, but it was no hardship. I had met a wonderful doula and aromatherapist by the name of Wende Sharma who would come with me to my appointments and sit with the girls. She did this several times and quickly became the first person outside our immediate family that Emmy took to. I had several appointments in a short time span, so they got to know her fairly well.

My first appointment was for a fetal echo and Level Two ultrasound. It was scheduled for early in the morning so I was still very tired. But you were feeling feisty, Stormie, kicking and punching me as I got dressed.

I heard a knock as I pulled my shirt over my head.

"Hey, Wende," I said, answering the door. "Thanks again for coming with me today. It's such a big help."

"No problem," she said, scooping Emmy into her arms,

looking down at Anne who had wrapped herself around Wende's leg. "Let's get you two ready."

Wende stood at a short four feet, ten inches, her silver and brown hair falling just below her shoulders. She always looked well put together, dressed in long skirts and flowing shirts every time I saw her. She had a carefree attitude about life and every time the girls and I were with her, everything seemed better.

We drove to the doctor's practice and talked about you the entire way there, Stormie. Wende had told me repeatedly how brave I was for rearranging everything in my life to make sure you had the best.

We arrived a few minutes early so Emmy, Anne, and Wende settled themselves in the waiting room while I went to check in.

The ultrasound technician was very pleasant, and even warmed the gel so it would be more comfortable for both of us. However, the second the transducer touched my belly you went wild, rolling, twisting, and kicking. You kicked so hard that the technician lost his grip on the wand, sending it flying to the floor.

"Wow!" he said. "She's a feisty one, huh? Strong. Determined."

I laughed. "That she is."

"They're the ones that always do the best," he said.

"You're not the first person to tell me that." I smiled to myself. It was one of the few times since the technician at Hartford Hospital had pulled me aside that I had heard anything positive about you come from the mouth of someone in the medical field.

When he was finished, I met with the pediatric cardiologist. I was nervous and afraid of what she was going to say. The prognosis at Yale had left me with the impression that you were going to need surgery to transform your heart into a single ventricle. I was curious when the doctor pulled out a heart diagram that seemed very different.

"The good news is that I do believe we can handle the heart defects that your baby has. I see that you were advised that she will probably need a single ventricle repair, but I don't think that is the case. I'm seeing some septal tissue here that indicates she may be a good candidate for bi-vent repair."

This was breathtaking news, Stormie, and from there it only got better. The prognosis with a bi-vent repair was significantly better than with a single ventricle, and there was a good chance you would need fewer operations.

As I exited the clinic I called my mother and Rachel. I tried to keep my voice as calm as possible. "They said... they said she... she will probably be able to have a bi-vent!"

We were all very excited. Over the next few appointments that enthusiasm grew. I met with the geneticist and the high risk doctor's office shortly after and the appointments went wonderfully. The geneticist talked me out of the amnio, which I had been certain was going to be something they would suggest. I had been having second thoughts about having it done after hearing how long the results would take, and that it might not even find anything. The geneticist reminded me that the procedure for genetic testing was quick and easy once you were born, so there was no need to rush.

She also preliminarily diagnosed you with Agenesis of the Corpus Callosum, a rare birth defect in a part of the brain that allows the two hemispheres to communicate with each other. The implications of that were absolutely impossible to tell, with cases existing where an individual had no resulting detriment to brain function, ranging up to possible learning and developmental delays. While this was not absolution of a brain problem like I had hoped, it wasn't something that was a death sentence either, and it was even fairly mild in the scope of brain abnormalities.

With all the different issues you had developed, the hospital required that I see the high risk doctors. Even though my pregnancy was progressing normally, they were concerned about your welfare and thought it best to do all the pregnancy care with doctors who were a little more accustomed to dealing with complicated pregnancies. I was not happy about that designation, as I had worked with many different high risk families, and the designation of high risk often meant there was a much greater push for invasive tests and procedures that I did not necessarily want. I wanted to continue the pregnancy as normally as possible, and there was no indication as to any reason that I shouldn't. You were doing well in utero and I was gaining enough weight and eating well. With the exception of the defects, we were mutually healthy.

My first conversation with the high risk doctors at the University of Michigan's women's hospital really set my mind at ease. There were no alarmists telling me that I had to have a C-Section because of your heart, nor was there a push for invasive testing or any more testing than absolutely necessary. They were open-minded enough to agree that I didn't need to be tested for gestational diabetes or be placed on any restricted activity.

I was so thankful, Stormie. The best part of my conversation with the doctors was when we talked about my birth plan. As a doula, I had very specific ideas of what I wanted. I was afraid that an epidural would do you more harm during the birthing process or the time shortly after birth, and therefore I was looking to explore every possible means for myself to have adequate support and resources for pain management. I wanted to labor in a tub, and I didn't want anything artificial used in the delivery process. One obstetrician had mentioned that I should deliver in an operating room, to eliminate any emergent situation if you were born needing additional resources that were not available in the low risk rooms. But they were fine with letting me labor in a low risk room with a tub and then moving to an operating room when the appropriate time came. They knew I would have at least one doula, perhaps two, and were supportive of this as well as my wish to keep the placenta without having any treatments done to it in pathology. It was astounding to me that such a big teaching hospital was so open to naturalistic ideas and practices. They were so supportive of my wishes, a practice unknown to me from my experience with other hospitals.

After meeting all the doctors and specialists, I finally got a chance to meet the woman who had helped me to put it all together. Sally, the cardiac social worker who had helped to coordinate my appointments, was very obviously in support of my decision to carry you and bring you into the world. We had several long discussions about things I'm sure she never talked to other patients about, such as patient rights, parenting topics, the care of special needs children, government, and the views of the practitioners in the hospital. She told me that Ann Arbor was considered a mecca of liberal views in a very conservative state. I was very happy to hear that, Stormie. It seemed I had chosen the best place to give birth. We had a lot in common when it came to our personal interests, so what started as a conversation about some aspect of the pregnancy or your care, usually turned into a long discussion about something else. I was glad to have her around and felt I could trust her to help me get the best for you.

A few days after my first appointment, Herb called with a request. "I want you to meet up with Sally and sign a release of information for the intended parents."

"Why?" I asked. "The Stones can't get to me here, right?"

"They can't pursue litigation here," he clarified, "but they can still cause trouble, and as the genetic father, Mr. Stone will have to sign over his parental rights in order to allow the adoption to go through. I don't foresee that being a problem, but we should be prepared. They have already been in contact asking for your medical information from February and beyond. I think we can placate them by giving them access to the newer test results, but we'll have to act quickly since we want to have it all settled before the baby is born."

The Stones were understandably upset that I had left Connecticut. I hadn't exactly been forthcoming with my plans to move. They also hadn't asked, or made any indication that they wanted to know, what my plans were. Under the laws there, they had control over the situation. Moving to Michigan changed the whole game plan.

Since that day at Hartford Hospital the Stones had shown only minimal interest in the pregnancy. Their calls had stopped, and according to the hospital records I was collecting, they weren't calling the specialists I saw to get any information about what we were seeing that was going to ultimately affect you. From what I saw and what I heard from the lawyers, they were angry that I had not terminated, but they had not shown the slightest interest in any further resolution. Herb had passed on to their lawyer the news of my decision to give you up for adoption, but we never heard any response back. Sharon had told me I was on my own, and if that meant that you were going to end up in state custody, then I was going to step in and make sure that didn't happen. And yet I understood how this would make the Stones feel. I took their power away from them and made them defenseless in the situation they had intended to command. It was heartbreaking, but it was also very angering, and it was incomprehensible to me that they could walk away so easily.

On several occasions I sat on the couch in my apartment in Michigan wondering what Roger and Ursula were doing. Did they think about how you were or whether you were as strong and feisty as I knew you were? Did they wrestle with the idea that they had wanted to wipe out your life? Did they wonder what would happen to you? I am sure that they did, and I am sure that this was a very difficult task for a woman who had so desperately wanted you to be the perfect addition to her family. She was grieving that perfect baby, and the loss of a dream is a very hard thing to endure, especially when it is so close, then slips away.

Sitting on the couch with my laptop resting on my thighs, I paged through comment after comment online. The surrogacy community seemed evenly divided, some supporting my decision and others adamantly opposing what I had done. Word had rapidly spread about our situation, Stormie. As you can imagine, my choice to relocate and have you in Michigan had caused a minor uproar. I closed the screen and stared out the window, startled a moment later when my phone rang.

"Crystal, do you have a Facebook page on which you share information about the baby?" Mr. Herb Brail asked.

"Well... kind of."

"I'm going to need you to take it down. Right now."

> There are very few human beings who receive the truth, complete and staggering, by instant illumination. Most of them aquire it fragment by fragment.
>
> —Anais Nin

CHAPTER TWENTY-FOUR
May 30, 2012

I **had to stay in the shadows.** Ursula Stone had somehow gained access to the group I formed on Facebook and found the ultrasound picture I posted of your open hands. During the last ultrasound in Connecticut, the doctor was very concerned that your hands were in tight fists, a possible characteristic of neurological defects. I was so elated to have a copy of your picture from my ultrasound in Michigan with your fingers outstretched that I shared it within the group.

I never thought I did anything wrong by posting it, but apparently Roger and Ursula were furious. A letter from their lawyer soon came through Michael. As I opened it, I could feel a nauseous sensation rise in the pit of my stomach and travel up to my throat. I fought the urge to throw up, took a deep breath, and began to read the letter:

Dear Attorney Brail,

Before responding to your letter of May 25, I must protest the outrageous audacity of Ms. Kelley, to be posting ultrasound pictures of the fetus on Facebook. I cannot even begin to say how abusive and insensitive her postings are, given the extremely delicate nature of this matter. Paragraph 20 of the Gestational Surrogacy Agreement requires that all parties 'Shall not provide information to the public, news media, or any other person regarding his or her involvement in the surrogacy process.' Please have Ms. Kelley remove all Facebook and other postings which in any way reference this surrogacy or this pregnancy, forward to me a list of all such posts, and let me know as soon as they have been removed.

In response to your comments of May 25, I can assure you that my clients are not 'Attempting to thwart the adoption plan or place [your] client in a disadvantageous position by pursuing litigation.' My clients simply need to safeguard their only interest; the only party who had disregarded her obligations throughout this entire transaction has been Ms. Kelley who was not truthful in her application to Surrogacy International and who, in further point of fact, decided to continue this pregnancy only after my clients refused Ms. Kelley's demand for a substantial sum of money in order to terminate it! And now, of course, Ms. Kelley has chosen to make a graphic post on the internet. My clients are understandably reluctant to take her at her word at this juncture. If we can agree upon a plan, then my clients will forego their litigation options. If we cannot agree, then my clients will pursue every avenue available to them.

It would go a long way to demonstrate Ms. Kelley's good faith for her to authorize you to accept service of the Connecticut action on her behalf. The documents are attached for your review. My client's cooperation also requires the access to medical records and providers that I have previously discussed along with full and complete details of the adoption plan, including the prospective adoptive parents' dossier. The sooner they receive this information the sooner we can move forward.

I look forward to hearing from you again soon.

My ears burned and my eyes began to narrow, creating a tunnel-like illusion, darkening the perimeter of my vision. A clause in the surrogacy agreement? Litigation? Against me? Why?

I pulled out my contract and sure enough the clause was there. I hadn't remembered reading it, nor did I think that I was exploiting anything. But fine, I had to stay dark until they signed the papers to relinquish their parental rights. The litigation was different, though. It was what Michael and I had feared in Connecticut and it seemed as though our fears were coming true.

Herb explained that they were only seeking to have their own names placed on the birth certificate instead of mine. But they were going about doing that in the state of Connecticut and not Michigan. It was very confusing, as state laws and state judgments are autonomous of each other. Just as marriage laws vary from state to state, the same holds true for surrogacy. A ruling made in the state of Connecticut would have no bearing on the application of the law in Michigan. A state cannot authorize a birth certificate for a citizen who was not born there. So there was little to no chance that a judge would grant any motion. Yet we would still have to deal with the threat of litigation as we moved forward with the adoption plans.

Herb had quickly compiled a response to the Stones' lawyer, and it was every bit as intimidating as the letter we had received. He wasn't going to back down and that was clear in his response.

Letter to the Stones' Lawyer:

In light of the circumstances between the respective parties arising from the gestational surrogacy contract, any adverse litigation would be ill-advised. Although you stated during our phone conversation on May 16, 2012, that the agreement contained a choice of law provision for Connecticut, any such judgment rendered in that state is highly unlikely to be recognized by Michigan in light of the Surrogate Parenting Act.

Given the intention of both of our clients not to parent the expected child, the most rational resolution is obviously the termination of all parental rights and adoptive placement. The statement that your clients 'do not consent to any such placement' is inexplicable. What precisely are your clients' intentions regarding custody and care of the expected child?

Your statements regarding obligations under the agreement are essentially moot in light of what has transpired prior to my involvement and the governing law in Michigan regarding surrogacy contracts. I am more than willing to share medical information prior to the birth of the child to confirm the abnormalities presently existing in the fetus and expected medical prognosis, but not under the threat of litigation based on a contract that is void and unenforceable as contrary to public policy in the State of Michigan.

I propose the following:

1. The Stones abstain from pursuing any litigation arising from the gestational surrogacy contract.

2. Medical information is exchanged regarding the fetus.

3. Parental rights of the mother (Kelley), the putative father (R. Stone), and to whatever extent parental rights of the biological mother (U. Stone) are recognized by Michigan are terminated under the Michigan Adoption Code and the child placed for adoption.

4. Mutual and reciprocal releases of all claims are executed between Stones and Kelley.

I have been engaged in adoption and assisted reproductive technology cases for the past thirty years in Michigan so I do have more than a passing familiarity with the issues presented by my client.

Before sending the letter Herb suggested that we cooperate with the demands of the Stones. If we gave them what they wanted, then they would hopefully work with us and we could have all the paperwork filled out before the court date was set.

■　■　■

The next morning one of my doula contacts came over to my house. As we talked about your future, Stormie, the doorbell rang. I excused myself from the kitchen table and walked towards the front of the house. I opened the door and saw a petite woman who looked

to be in her mid-twenties. She introduced herself as a messenger
from Herb's office and handed me the medical releases and other
paperwork. I invited her in and offered her some iced tea.

"It seems like you two have a lot to discuss," the doula said,
"I'm going to leave you alone."

"Thanks for stopping over," I said, squeezing her hand as I
walked her to the front door.

The messenger then handed me a large manila envelope.
"Herb sent me to give these to you."

"Oh, thanks. Come. We can sit in the kitchen and go over
everything."

The petite woman followed me inside then sat down near the
window.

"So," I began, opening the envelope to reveal a stack of
papers, "you work for Herb?"

"I'm a law student actually. Learning the ropes. My name's
Alexis."

"Nice to meet you, Alexis. I'm Crystal."

"I've heard all about your story as a surrogate. I can't believe
everything that's happened."

The young woman and I spent a while talking about the case
and Herb's part in making the adoption plan a reality. We discussed
the psychological implications of surrogacy and the need for
regulations and laws regarding cases like mine when things went
wrong.

"There's far too much opportunity for disaster with the
way the current system is structured," she said, taking a sip of
tea. "When the ethics of abortion interweave with the personal
feelings of attachment, protection, personal responsibility, and
even ownership, it's often to the detriment of the psychologically

disadvantaged pregnant women." My new friend shook her head in disgust. "It's like they think they own that baby."

Her sentiment was not lost on me. "They paid for the baby to be created, they paid for the baby to be implanted, and if they own the baby then in their eyes I stole her."

"But they made it clear they didn't want her. Why couldn't they just make up their minds and leave you alone from there?"

"I don't know," I said, filling up her glass with ice and more tea. "Maybe they feel some type of responsibility. Maybe they changed their minds. I can't try to tell you what must have been going on in their heads, but they seem to have made the decision to regain control, even if they have little to no chance of achieving their goal with the way they went about it."

My visitor scrunched up her forehead and slammed the palm of her hand on the table. "So what the heck do they want?"

"They aren't saying. On one hand they want information and their names on the birth certificate, hence the lawsuit. And on the other hand they say they aren't trying to negate the adoption plan. Who knows? All I know is if their intention is to make this super stressful and potentially do harm to the baby, they've got that covered."

"I can't believe these people," she said, her face twisted in anguish. "How selfish can you be? Either give the kid up or take care of her! They need to make up their freaking minds. This baby's not a used car. You can't say 'Oh, I don't want her. Wait! I only want her if she isn't too broken.'"

"I know."

"And apparently that's what the plan was before," she said.

I looked at her. I was shocked, Stormie. I could not believe what I was hearing. This news was knocking the stuffing out of me.

"Seriously?" I said as my world began to topple out of control, "I thought they wanted to give her to the state?"

"I don't know. I didn't get the whole story, but apparently they thought that the safe-haven law would give them enough time to see if they could deal with taking care of her, and if not they'd dump her off on someone else. It was pretty obvious that they didn't want you to have her. I only heard Ursula make mention of you once, but when she did she sounded crazy. You could hear the hate in her voice. I don't know why. You solved their problem for them."

"So you think they were going to take her for a test drive first?"

"They couldn't stand to let you have her, Crystal. That must be what this is about. It's about control. You hold all the cards, so now they need to do something to challenge your authority on the situation. They have to keep you in the dark so they can plot whatever little game they plan on playing to keep the upper hand." She took a swig of her drink and continued, almost as though she was the injured party. "It's like your baby is a box, and they paid for the box so they see it as their box. But you have it. They don't want it, but you can't have it either, because then they aren't in control of their box. It's ridiculous. I can't believe people still think that way. A baby isn't a box!" The ice in her glass clanked as she whipped the glass around in the air, her voice growing louder and louder and more and more vehement.

To calm her nerves—and mine—I suggested we get on with the matter at hand. We went over the case details for an affidavit and some other documents that Michael would present in Connecticut court. When we were finished going over everything, she stood up and thanked me for my hospitality.

"Wow! I've been here for a long time. I should get back to the office before I get into trouble."

"Thanks for bringing everything over," I said, unable to express to her the full extent of my gratitude.

"Of course," she said, reaching for the front door. She hesitated, turning back to look at me. "It makes me so mad. These people wanted a baby so badly that they paid you to carry it for them. But because she isn't perfect they wanted to give up on her. Why couldn't they just give up, then—give up and leave you alone? It's not like you're running off to give birth in the woods and leave the baby to die. You've done everything possible to make sure that this child has a stable and loving home once she's born. Heck, even if you decided to keep her, at least you are willing to take on the responsibility without hesitation. But they would never leave you alone if you tried to keep her. And why do they care? They didn't want her after they found out she was going to be different."

"I wish I could answer that," I said. "If you find the answer though, I'd love to hear it."

■ ■ ■

The last month of my pregnancy dragged on, leaving me feeling more alone than I ever had before. Apart from you and my girls, Stormie, I was separated from the rest of the world. Without my access to the online group, and even though the girls were with me, I felt isolated. I wasn't sleeping well, often lying awake at night thinking about the situation, wishing there was an easier solution. With no case law to base Michael's belief that it would be thrown out, the stress of the litigation threat became immense.

The first court date passed and was rescheduled for another date. Based on many different factors, Michael entered a motion to dismiss. He was confident that the case would continue until after you were born, therefore negating any chance of the motion for the Stones to be named on the birth certificate. However, that meant we were running against the clock.

As if my stress level wasn't high enough, Anne was testing my patience more and more every day. When I found her for the third morning in a row, hiding under her bed with several of my fruit baskets and boxes of crackers, I almost lost my temper. Without my online support I didn't know where to turn, so I called my mother. She suggested that she take Anne to St. Louis with her until it was time for your birth.

It was very hard for me to send her away. As my first child she had always been more independent than Emmy, but no less my baby. No matter how annoyed I was with her behavior, I was love-struck by my daughter and cherished her presence in my world, but I needed a break. I cried the day I brought her to the airport in Detroit to meet my mother on a quick turnaround flight back to St. Louis. She was excited to see Grandma and go on a vacation with her.

After dropping her off, Emmy and I returned to the quiet apartment—alone, apart from your very prominent presence.

It was two weeks until my due date and I didn't know what to do with myself. My apartment was immaculately clean and everything was ready for your arrival. I hadn't gathered much in the way of baby equipment because we knew you would stay in the hospital at first, and I figured Rachel had most of the things you would need.

With the time that we had, Emmy and I took a lot of walks

and did a whole bunch of art projects. We tie-dyed cloth diapers in the hope that they would get some use with you, and made arrangements with the doula and photographer. All my birth attendants were volunteering their time and I was very thankful for their services. Ashley had done maternity photo shoots already and I was excited for the birth shoot. My bags were packed and I was ready long before the big day came.

I don't know
how to defend
myself: surprised
innocence cannot
imagine being
under suspicion.

—Pierre Corneille

CHAPTER TWENTY-FIVE
June 12, 2012

I sat impatiently by the window, hoping to catch a glimpse of Scott's car as it pulled into the parking lot behind my building. They were supposed to have left Connecticut in the early morning, which meant they should be arriving at any time.

Scott and I had been getting along pretty well. From past experience I knew he was very attracted to me in my pregnant state, and I always felt better about myself and my body with child, so it suited us to be together during my pregnancy. We hadn't been able to see each other in person in two months and spent our time talking on a webcam or Android app. In our last chat Scott expressed how happy he was to be coming to see me and the girls in Michigan. Emmy couldn't wait for her dad to arrive but thankfully was fast asleep, taking her usual nap for the day. Anne was with my mom and had planned on joining us once you were born.

I was equally as excited to see my father who was making the journey with Scott. Not only that, but though I considered myself to be an independent person, there were still some things I would rather let a man do. In my pregnant state that list of things was a bit longer than usual and it had been neglected without someone around to oblige my needs. My father had also promised to keep the girls at my apartment while I was in the hospital with you, Stormie.

In the two weeks leading up to your birth I began to feel an increased amount of pressure. With both the girls I'd had long and tiring labors, thirty-seven and forty-five hours respectively. I had to prepare for another long and tiring ordeal.

Emmy woke up before Scott and my dad arrived so we decided to take a walk. The weather was hot and it was hard to stay hydrated. With each step I felt my stomach tighten up, then loosen. It repeated several times and I had to sit down more than once. Emmy didn't mind; she wandered around or sat next to me, a stark contrast to the way she behaved under the influence of Anne.

"Mommy okay?" she asked, smiling up at me.

"Yes, Honey. Mommy is fine," I said as another wave passed.

Ever since before we moved I had been practicing my Hypnobabies relaxation techniques, so I was well prepared and able to cope fairly easily with the contractions as they came. The contractions grew stronger and I told Emmy to get into the stroller so we could head home. As we approached the long driveway that led to the back of our building a black car drove past and the driver's side window rolled down.

"Hey there, pretty lady. Need a ride?"

"Daddy!" Emmy squealed out.

As I helped Scott get his bags from the car, I noticed his finger was in a splint. He laughed at me when he saw me staring at his middle finger covered in a thick white bandage.

"Well, I thought if I had to hurt myself I might as well get some people angry," he said, his face deadpan. "That's what I get for working too hard for the man. Damn tire bit me!"

I chuckled. Scott always had this way of telling stories that made even the most gruesome acts sound ridiculous and funny. I didn't want to admit that I had missed his crazy humor, but it was nice to have him in front of me, cracking his odd jokes again.

The passenger door opened, my father grunting as he hoisted himself out of the car. He looked disheveled. His shirt was a wrinkled mess and his hair looked as if he had just woken up from a long sleep.

"Fun ride, Dad?" I asked him.

"Oh my God, Crystal. Does he always drive like that?" He looked at me with wide eyes. "I had to hold on to the 'oh shit' handle just to keep from saying oh shit the whole ride!"

I laughed out loud. Scott chuckled and put his arm around me. "He kept saying we were in no rush. But I wanted to get here. I missed you and the girls." As he bent over to hug Emmy I caught a glimpse of the man who had captured my heart more than five years ago, and it brought tears to my eyes. He stood up and kissed me on the cheek. "Come on," he said. "Let's go inside."

■   ■   ■

In the days that followed we took long walks and strolled the campus. We also had the chance to visit some of the museums, libraries, and playgrounds in the area. At night we sat on my couch and relaxed as a family.

Scott came with me to my final two doctors' appointments and got to meet the social worker, geneticist, and a few of the doulas I had been working with.

One morning I had a doula friend come over and sit with Emmy while Scott and I walked the seven blocks to the hospital. I was scheduled for a non-stress test. It was a standard practice for babies with heart problems.

You were apparently very sleepy from the walk, Stormie, and you didn't really move around much. The nurse wasn't concerned, but she went to get me a glass of juice to see if we could stimulate you into action for a biophysical profile. While she was gone the social worker slipped into the room.

"I want you to know, Crystal, that Mrs. Stone has been calling repeatedly trying to get information about you and the baby."

What the heck can she want to know now? I wondered.

"She's been asking about the heart condition, and if it means that you will have to be induced or have a C-Section."

"Great," Scott said, not missing a beat in the conversation. "They'd better not show up here and try to make trouble. I'll have no problem showing them exactly where the door is."

"Well, we're a little concerned," the social worker said. "She has gone to great lengths to get this information. We feel it might be in your best interests to discuss keeping you here under confidentiality once the baby is born."

"How do we do that?" I asked. "They have my release. I can't keep anything from them."

"There is one way."

The social worker suggested I use an alias or appear as a

Jane Doe so I couldn't be identified in the computer system. It would help to keep my records private—and yours, Stormie—and once you were born the only information they would have access to would be the records prior to my admittance. It sounded like a good option, so we began to set up the paperwork to make it happen.

The nurse reappeared with my juice. "So, what are your plans for when the baby comes? Do you have someone to stay with your children?" she asked. "I see that your husband is in town, but for how long?"

I laughed, taking a sip of my drink. "He's not my husband. But he'll be here for the birth. Or at least, we hope he will. He's supposed to leave a week from Friday."

"And the childcare situation?"

I explained that my dad was also visiting and my mother would be arriving as soon as I told her it was time.

"Oh, okay," she responded, a hesitancy in her voice.

"Something wrong?" I asked.

"No. Certainly not. It's just that babies have a way of coming when they want to and I hope your mother gets here in time for the birth."

My stomach suddenly tightened and a moment of nausea washed over me. The pressure combined with your relentless kicking forced me to lie back on the table.

"Been having those a lot?"

"All the time for the last two weeks."

"Looks like you're about ready. That was definitely a real contraction."

"I know but they're not quite strong enough yet. I've done this before and typically I have long labors and quick deliveries."

The social worker and the technician looked at each other,

then the technician excused herself and closed the door behind her. The social worker rolled a chair over towards me, her hands folded in her lap.

"I don't want to scare you, and I know you're planning on a totally natural birth for Stormie, but I think you need to take into consideration that you are, technically, in labor. We could admit you now. You have what could possibly be a real time issue if you don't have this baby in the next few days, and I don't want to see you stuck in your house, waiting for a babysitter, then giving birth in your living room. If you have fast deliveries we need to make sure you are as close to the hospital as possible all the time."

"I only live seven blocks away. I walk here almost every day."

"I don't think we really want to take that chance. This baby has some serious health concerns. She isn't like the normal baby where if she's born in the back of the car on the way to the hospital it will be okay. We won't really know what we're dealing with until she gets here. And we don't want this baby to be born outside of the hospital. It's your decision, but please think about scheduling a time to come in so we can speed up your labor a little bit and get her here safely."

If Scott and my dad were not still here, I didn't know who would keep Emmy when I had to be admitted to the hospital, and I didn't have any way to predict when it would happen so that I could plan ahead. I couldn't leave Emmy alone with someone she didn't really know.

"You're right," I said. "I should think about that."

"Just give us a call when you decide," she said, exiting the room.

As Scott and I walked out to the car to go home, the pressure waves picked up significantly, and then slowed down as we got closer to the apartment.

"Do you really want to be by yourself when you realize it's time?" Scott asked.

I didn't respond. There was too much buzzing around in my head to think about and I didn't know what to say.

Scott and I walked inside and I went to the bedroom to lie down and think about my options. I fell back onto the bed, my shoes still on my feet, and after a few moments I decided to give one of my doulas, Jen Henderson, a shot at helping me get things going.

She arrived a half-hour later with another doula, and while we chatted they palpitated my belly. We determined that you were in the posterior position so I had to do certain things to encourage you to turn. I was certain this was what was keeping us from progressing past the tedious prodromal labor I was experiencing.

I made an appointment for the following morning to see a chiropractor who was experienced in the Webster technique, a method sometimes used for turning breech or posterior babies, and scheduled another doula to come over and help me try some positions to get you to settle into the birth position.

You were stubborn, Stormie—I did everything I possibly could to get you to rotate. The time was quickly approaching where I would have to deal with the reality that either I was going to help my labor along, or I was going to have to face the possibility that I would be in labor without Scott or my dad around.

The chiropractic treatment worked immediately, but only a few hours passed before you flipped yourself around once again. The sporadic but strong pressure waves continued to come. I began to get very frustrated. Finally I called the social worker.

"All right." I told her. "I'll come in to move this along. It's not like we don't know she's ready. I've been having real contractions for weeks."

"Sometimes scheduling is the best thing," she said. "When dealing with babies with such uncertainty coming in to the world, knowing that the resources are available and ready can mean the difference between a good experience and one that's rushed or emergent. And we're sure of her dates so we're comfortable that she's ready. Let's schedule an induction for this coming Friday."

"Sounds good," I sighed.

By 5 p.m. that night my mother had a flight and Rachel was in the car on her way to Michigan. She was going to wait for our call at a friend's house nearby so that she could be present at the hospital when her new daughter was born.

JUNE 22, 2012

As soon as I arrived at the hospital on Friday night, the waves started to pick up again.

"Maybe that's why we haven't progressed," I said to Scott. "I've been stressing about not being at home when she's born and it's been keeping her in."

"I don't think that's the reason she's not here yet, Crystal."

We set up the room while we waited for the doctor to come and talk to us. I had decided that I wanted to start with a drug called Cervadil, which would help me to dilate before the use of Pitocin. I had a client once whose water had broken and she had successfully used Cervadil to kick-start labor. I knew it didn't work for everyone, but I still wanted to avoid Pitocin unless it was absolutely necessary to get things going. I remembered the intensity of those induced contractions during Anne's birth, and this time, to safeguard your health, I was determined to forego an epidural. When it came down to your best interests, Stormie, I didn't want a lethargic or sleepy baby who might not have the energy to thrive.

However, the Cervadil was not successful in getting me any further into labor, and then there was another complication. On the overnight shift Friday evening into Saturday morning, a baby was born with significant heart issues. The cardiac NICU team decided that they were not adequately staffed to care for two brand new heart babies. They asked the obstetrician's office to move my induction to Monday morning when they would have a full staff again.

I was so upset. I was ready to give birth, and once again I was being pushed back and told I couldn't do what for so long I had been preparing myself to do.

The moment I walked out of the hospital, the waves I had been feeling for the previous two weeks stopped. My body went into defense mode, and no matter how much I tried to re-start what had already been happening, it simply was not going to work. Even though I was frustrated, I decided to enjoy the last few days of pregnancy. I called Ashley and scheduled one last photography session. We agreed to meet at my apartment, then walk over to a nearby arboretum. There was a river about an hour's walk away and the path around it circled to the hospital, then back towards my apartment. It would serve as the perfect setting for one last photo shoot. We spent the afternoon walking the windy trail down by the river and back up to my apartment. It was so nice to just exist as a family.

When I went back to the hospital on Sunday night, I was more than ready to meet you, Stormie. Once again the moment I entered the maternity ward my body began to tense and contract.

In order to ensure that there was adequate staffing present, the doctors didn't want to start a Pitocin drip until midnight. While we waited, Scott and I watched a movie. I found myself closing my eyes several times when stronger contractions overcame me. There were many times before midnight arrived when I had to concentrate on my breathing to get through the pain. A nurse came in a few minutes after twelve o'clock and I asked her to go very slowly with the Pitocin. She agreed, and began the drip at the lowest setting.

I focused on my breathing and on the inspirational index cards spread throughout the room. Within an hour the contractions had increased in intensity, making lying on the bed almost unbearable. My doula and Ashley, my photographer, arrived shortly afterwards, just as I was getting into the bathtub to try to relieve some of the pressure. Scott had lit some candles in an attempt to relax me while soft music played in the background. Breathing through the tightening and releasing of my belly, I labored quietly for several hours, knowing that the moment my water broke I'd be in for an intense ride. Sure enough, a few minutes later I felt a sudden release. But the water became too hot and I needed to get out.

I eventually moved to the floor and labored on a peanut ball. It was the only respite I could find in the moments before you were born. Our nurse was nowhere to be found. Luckily, my doula had called the head nurse, and immediately medical staff streamed into the room to set up the warmer and prepare for you. People streamed into the room, setting up the warmer and preparing for you. Moments later a doctor arrived and told me to push. As you emerged into her hands you let out a loud cry. I was so overcome with relief that I collapsed to the floor and began to sob, knowing for sure you were as strong as I had thought you were.

The Pitocin did its job, and the Hypnobabies worked as
well. I still think that I experienced the least possible amount of discomfort while in labor with you. The ending was difficult, but in one way or another all births are. Seven hours after the first dose of Pitocin entered my bloodstream, you were catapulted into the world kicking and screaming. The timing was so close that the doctors almost missed your birth, and due to the commotion I wasn't able to remind anyone to delay clamping your cord. I still consider that was detrimental for you, since from the moment your body started to adjust to life outside the womb, your heart had to start working extra hard to keep you going.

You were pale, but you were breathing.

You were moving.

You were crying.

And oh yes, Stormie, from the very beginning you were making me proud.

Do what you
feel in your
heart to be
right—for you'll
be criticized
anyway.

—Eleanor
Roosevelt

CHAPTER TWENTY-SIX
June 29, 2012

I sat in your room, Stormie, resting in the small armchair with my eyes closed. The fabric covering the chair felt like plastic and the cushions hard, like sitting on stone. The beeping of the machines that monitored your heart rate, breathing, and other vital signs buzzed in the background. I opened my eyes, unable to relax. Why wasn't a nurse coming to change the medication dispenser?

I knew what the buzzing meant, but the nurse was nowhere to be seen. I started to walk out the entrance of the Isolette when the door to the Cardiac Intensive Care Unit swung open.

I froze.

Standing on the other side of the door talking to the security

officer at the desk were Roger and Ursula. I began to feel hot and
knew my blood pressure was rising. I took a deep breath in, trying
to alleviate the sour feeling building in the pit of my stomach.
Ursula looked towards the doors and saw me. She turned and
walked quickly in my direction, Roger a few short steps behind.

A nurse met her at the doorway. "I'm sorry, who are you? We
can't let in any unauthorized visitors."

"Get out of my way!" Ursula pushed her way past the nurse
and onto the floor of the Cardiac Intensive Care Unit. A guard in the
lobby stepped into view, walking out of the hallway to the right, but
I knew that Ursula would reach me long before he could.

Where is she?" she exclaimed as she pushed her way through
the doors. "Where is my baby? Who the hell do you think you are?
Get out of here! This is my baby. You stole her from us!"

"Someone. Please. Someone help me!" I called out.

But nobody came.

The floor was eerily quiet, save for one nurse sitting at the
nurses' station, working on a computer. She barely looked up as
Ursula stormed past her station and to the door of your Isolette. She
paused when I didn't move out of her way.

"You can't go in there." My voice was shaking.

"Like hell I can't! That's my baby. You signed that contract.
That is my child in there. Let me in there. I am her mother!"

Suddenly out of nowhere your nurse appeared. "I'm sorry,
Mrs. Stone, but I can't let you in there. Please lower your voice.
You're going to upset the baby."

Finally the guard showed up. He was accompanied by
another person. They got on either side of Ursula and grabbed her
by the arm. "You are not authorized to be in here. Please come
with us."

CHAPTER TWENTY-SIX

She struggled against their hold, and for a moment I thought she was going to attack someone. Perhaps she would direct her anger at me. It was hard to tell as she squirmed and kicked, attempting to free herself from their grasp.

As she continued to struggle, the guards questioned her. "How did you find her room number? Who gave you this information?"

She was screaming obscenities, threatening everyone around her. More and more people were coming to the aid of the security guard, when suddenly I heard, "I've got a gun!"

A weapon was brandished into the air and as the security doors closed, two shots rang out.

I jumped to my feet. My hands were shaking and my heart felt as if it would beat out of my chest. Sweat began to build on my forehead and upper lip. The sirens were going off in the hallway, but for me the only sound in the room was your oxygen monitor. People rushed past your door, and then your nurse walked in, adjusted the little band around your toe, and glanced over at me. "Rough night?" she asked. "You were yelling at someone in your sleep."

I began to blush. "I was?"

"Oh yeah. Sounded like quite the battle. You sure you're okay?"

"Yeah, I'm fine. You haven't heard from that other woman, Ursula Stone, have you?"

"No, Ma'am. Last I heard from her was a couple of days ago. I believe they told her she needed to stop calling all the time. It was getting a bit out of control."

■ ■ ■

You were only a few days old, and since your birth I had stopped allowing the Stones access to your files. I was tired of the games, Stormie, tired of the misleading information and threats designed to give them a means of entry to you while still allowing them to stand back and be indecisive. I was taking control of your life and your care while waiting for the adoption process to be completed. Up until this point I had been compliant with all their demands, as well as all their requests. Their only choice was to give up their parental rights, or come to Michigan and file for paternity. But the lengths that they went to—the phone calls to Billing asking medical questions and information leaking out by dispatch—it was all mind-blowing.

That Ursula was able to obtain your room number was astonishing to me and prompted a meeting with the heads of security. Thank goodness I had been away having lunch when Ursula called because I would most certainly have hung up on her.

And then they did the unthinkable; they forged a release allowing them information pertaining to your condition by changing the name of the patient so that it reflected your name instead of mine. As remarkable as that was, when it didn't work they sent an affidavit to the legal team from the IVF clinic stating that Mr. Stone's sperm was the material used to fertilize the egg, along with an anonymous egg donor.

Ursula wasn't even technically your biological mother.

This entire time we had been focusing on the fact that you were created from the biological material of the Stones, both Roger and Ursula. Ursula had always acted as if you were her biological child, made from her egg. I didn't recall our exact conversation, but in our very first meeting she had told me that the frozen embryos were 'her babies.' And at the ultrasound where the Stones originally asked me to abort, the doctor went through the age of egg retrieval and a whole lot of technical information about the creation of the embryo that resulted in you. However, this affidavit showed that our assumptions had been incorrect.

Stormie—you were in no way related to her.

It changed a lot of things. With Mrs. Stone's tie to you invalidated, that meant that there was only one signature that needed to be acquired in order to approve the adoption plan. There was really only one person who needed to make a decision. It was not Ursula, yet she was the one calling every day, she was the one pushing all the buttons and making the waves that were disrupting every moment of every day for me.

"This is absurd!" I shouted into the phone as Lisette tried to calm me down.

"I know. I know," she repeated. "All of it is so incomprehensible. I'm so sorry you have to deal with this now."

"I can't handle them anymore."

I promised to keep Lisette informed of the situation but couldn't stay on the phone any longer. With every passing second my anger intensified.

■ ■ ■

I understand now that it was an act of a desperate woman, but at the time it angered me immensely. The Stones had asked me to terminate your life, Stormie. You, who lay sleeping in your crib across the room from me. For most of the pregnancy they had acted uninterested in your welfare or mine. Aside from the initial inquiry to the geneticist at Hartford Hospital we had no indication that they had done any sort of research into what your diagnosis would mean after your birth. They received access to the results of tests that they had been legally contracted to pay for, but had not actually paid. They got weekly progress reports from my lawyers and had admission to the medical reports from every ultrasound. They gave no indication that they had any intention of helping me, or you, or allowing anyone else to assist you either.

When the hospital's legal team decided that the affidavit could be substituted for a court document establishing parentage for the reason of disclosing medical information, I felt so defeated. All Ursula needed was her husband's signature on the same form they had forged a few days before, and they had every piece of information they could possibly want about you.

I had lost my leverage. All that was left to do now was to wait. The worst part was that we still didn't know what they wanted to do, or where the litigation they had been threatening all along was going.

Were they going to come and try to fight me for you? Or would they decide that, as previously discussed, you were a 'lemon' and they would wash their hands of the situation?

I lived in constant fear that Ursula and Roger would suddenly appear and try to take you away from me. Herb assured me that this was not a possibility. Even though the hospital had broken the precedent rule for establishment of paternity, you were in my custody, and my care. Michigan law ruled that you would remain in my custody and care until any guardianship or paternity claims were decided upon. Of course, with the lack of rationality the Stones had exhibited in the days after your birth, I wasn't so sure you were safe. My mother and Rachel both agreed that we would stand watch in your room until a resolution was devised. That meant that one of us would be there at all hours of the night or day.

CHAPTER TWENTY-SIX

I rarely left your side in those first few weeks and I was there for all your major events: your first bath, your nasogastric intubation, learning how to feed you from the special bottles for cleft babies. I relished every moment we had together.

I pumped so I could give you breast milk. Sitting next to your crib I watched you sleep. As I studied your tiny face, even with all the wires and tubes connected to your little body, you seemed at peace.

You were never happy being left alone and quickly displayed the personality traits I had predicted in you when I was pregnant. You didn't whimper like the other newborns, you screamed. You screamed when you were upset, and that usually involved you not being swaddled to give you the feeling of security you had in my womb, or when the nurses bothered you. I always felt bad when you got introduced to a new nurse.

"It's all right. It's not you," I'd tell them as you screeched at the top of your lungs.

When you were awake you were only happy if you were being held, straining to look at whoever was holding you while chewing on the edge of your fuzzy owl blanket.

For the first three weeks of your life, while we waited and wondered with the attorneys playing all kinds of tricks to get the Stones to make their move, I took care of you. I held you and rocked you. I fed you and loved you, Stormie. I snuggled you when they came to draw your blood, and I shooed the nurses away while you were sleeping. I did everything a mother could do for her baby and I waited for the day when the storybook page would have a happy ending.

Most of all, I marveled at you and watched you blow away the doctors' expectations. They were all so happy that you were stable and holding your own so well. And when you were ten days old they even started talking about sending you home.

JULY 3, 2012

"Stormie's coming home! She's coming home! She's coming home!" I yelled, pacing around the apartment, gathering up clothes on the floor in a frantic attempt at sprucing up the house for your arrival.

Emmy followed close behind like a puppy begging for a treat, snatching the small socks I dropped along the way. My mind raced. I didn't know where to begin. I needed to make sure everything was perfect before I brought you home.

I called Stacy to tell her the news.

"Are you serious?" Stacy sounded as excited as I was. "Tell me what you need."

An hour later I fell exhausted onto my unmade bed. Even though I had organized the apartment into a far better state than it was, I still felt like I was living in a dream. In a matter of twelve hours I would bring you into my little apartment. You'd finally be here, Stormie. It seemed so strange, and so unexpected. I never thought you would leave the hospital just two weeks after you were born. It was like a dream come true, and yet it scared me to death.

Your feeding issues were still pretty pronounced so I would have to wake up every few hours to feed you. I wasn't quite sure how I would pump and feed you at the same time. The pump required both hands and your bottles were not the same as those of a typical child. You had to squeeze the bottle in order to let the liquid out, since your cleft didn't allow you to obtain sufficient suction through the nipple.

"I see some long nights ahead of us," I said to Emmy who smiled as she hopped around on the floor behind me. "Girl, you have no idea what's coming."

With the commotion of your delivery and our daily trips to the hospital, Emmy had been through a lot in the last couple of weeks before you came home, especially as she did not have Anne around. Anne was nine hundred miles away with my mother in St. Louis. However, through it all she had become more independent and adaptable, characteristics I wasn't used to seeing in her. Emmy loved you so much, Stormie. She would sit, patiently waiting while we stayed with you and occasionally I would even let her feed you. She took a daily nap in the hospital room and would only allow herself to fall asleep if her hand was on your crib.

Stacy stopped by a couple of hours later with a few of the items I had asked her to bring me.

"Hey, Crystal," she said, coming through my front door with several packages.

We went into the kitchen and set the bags on the table.

"Thanks for bringing me all this stuff," I said, pulling the Angelcare monitor out of the first bag. The monitor was one of the most important items I requested because it would tell me if you stopped breathing in the middle of the night. You had choked on your own tongue and drool before when I was visiting you, and your oxygen saturation level dropped, all of which terrified me.

"Here are the blankets, clothes, and some more breastfeeding supplies," Stacy said, unpacking it all for me.

I fumbled, looking for somewhere to put the things she had brought.

"So how are you feeling about everything?" she asked.

"I don't know. I'm excited, of course. But I'm a little worried and nervous too. I'd kind of written off the whole newborn thing."

Stacy laughed at me. "You're a doula and you don't want to have a newborn?"

I smiled. "No, of course I love newborns. I love all babies. I'm just not sure I have enough energy or financial resources for a third child."

As I continued on I began to feel sentimental and tears clouded my eyes. "I just don't want anything to happen to her. I don't even know if I can keep her safe while she's here. What if something happens when she's with me? I don't think I could live with myself if I took her home and something went wrong."

I walked over to my couch, Stacy following close behind me.

"It'll all be fine," she said.

"I'm afraid I'll get too attached and I won't want to give her to Rachel and her family. And what if the Stones come and decide to fight for what they think are their rights? Even if I wanted to give her up I wouldn't be able to without giving her directly to them."

You see, Stormie, I had held on to the idea that you were going home with Rachel and were not going to be my responsibility forever, but when it came down to it I felt that way because I knew Rachel's home was the best place for you. Deep in my heart I still wanted to be your mother, and I still longed for the sweet cries of you waking up in the middle of the night next to me.

Emmy climbed on top of my lap. "Baby here?" she asked.

I took a deep breath and remembered what I had told myself a thousand times already. I knew it wouldn't be fair to Anne and Emmy for me to be so involved with another child. I had to be honest with myself. I could barely deal with the responsibility of two children with the amount of stress I was under. Your care would be something that would cause me constant worry, even more so if the Stones decided to try and exercise their wishes on your care. Regardless of whatever I felt about my own hopes to watch you grow up, I had to continue to tell myself that by allowing you to join Rachel's family I was doing what was best for you.

"No, Honey," I said, running my fingers through her hair. "Baby's not here. She's sleeping now."

■   ■   ■

The next morning I went to the hospital early while Emmy stayed with my sister at the apartment. It was Bethany's last day in town and we were going to go to the Children's museum before your discharge. Rachel and I talked on the way to see you and she assured me that she would be close by when we were sent home.

"I'll be here if you need me to help take care of her," she said. "It's whatever you want, Crystal."

When I arrived in your room I learned that Ursula and Roger were being most uncooperative with my efforts to get you out of the hospital. When Ursula heard that we were scheduled to go home, she called all the lawyers and hospital representatives that she could to halt the process. She reported to the hospital social worker that she was concerned about my stability and capability to properly care for you and tried to get the lawyers to issue an emergency custodial placement for you with Rachel. The stall tactic was fruitless, but it was enough to keep me from taking you home. The head of the department met with me the afternoon of your discharge, citing that you were not gaining enough weight for them to be comfortable with your discharge. Later we discovered this was a departmental decision made on the basis of the commotion caused by Ursula's interference.

A few days later a new doctor decided you were ready to go home, and again the discharge was rescinded at the last moment.

In the meantime, the lawyers were working on getting the adoption proceedings set up, but it was pointless without any sort of indication from the Stones that they were going to cooperate. The lawyers' inquiries to opposing counsel were most often ignored, or brushed aside with noncommittal responses. While we hoped they were just having difficulty with the decision, we also had to face the reality that Mr.. Stone may have been pursuing litigation in Michigan to establish paternity, which would put me in the precarious situation of giving him complete control, or fighting him for parental rights.

Herb gave them many opportunities to relinquish their rights, and asked many times what their intentions were, without response.

I never did get to bring you home.

A FEW DAYS LATER

Late one evening, as I was sitting at home with Emmy, I received a phone call. Herb wanted to inform me of the court date that would occur the following week.

"Is it actually going to do anything?" I asked.

"There's a good chance we'll be forced to continue on with this process while we serve Mr.. Stone with paternity paperwork," he replied. "But if they do sign the paperwork and get it to me in time, then we'll be able to complete everything that day."

He quickly explained how Michigan handled adoption

cases. Unlike in many other states, parental rights to the child were terminated by the state of Michigan on the day the paperwork was signed. There was no waiting period, and no time where I could change my mind and get you back if I wanted to. While that was something that made me very sad, I realized it also meant that once Mr.. Stone signed the papers, he had the same limitation and therefore would not be able to put me in a situation where he could retain his parental rights and I could not. Considering the secrecy the Stones had shown thus far, I was extremely paranoid that they would act in some way to put me at a disadvantage.

Days passed without any word. Rachel and I took turns at your hospital bedside, feeding you and hoping you would gain enough weight for the doctors to tell us we could actually take you outside. We diapered you and comforted you after all the nurse's tests and prods, and we even replaced your nasogastric tube when you pulled it out. We talked with doctors and nurses about the best course for your care and discussed where things were headed between us.

Rachel and I developed a bond through the course of the many hours we spent by your side. We were essentially trapped in stasis, waiting for an answer that might never come.

JULY 11, 2012

As hard as it was to get through those last few days, we did it. And then the momentous morning came when I had to appear in court.

I woke up nervous, immediately nauseous and unsure of myself. According to the voicemail I received the night before, Herb still had not garnered any paperwork from the Stones, even though their lawyer assured us it was in the mail. My heart raced with the prospect of going to court to ask a judge to demand that Mr.. Stone establish paternity. I had a feeling it would cause an uproar I did not really want to face.

I got out of bed and immediately went to take a shower. As the water fell onto my body I moved my hands to my stomach, remembering what it had felt like when you moved inside me. I missed the protective control I had before you were born, when only I could keep you safe, sheltered from everyone who doubted you.

I ran my hands through my hair and stared into the stream, wondering what our lives would be like if I kept you. I knew in my heart that I would never be able to give you everything you needed.

I washed the soap off my body and out of my hair, then grabbed my towel as I stepped out of the shower, catching a glimpse of my body in the mirror above the sink. My stomach had shrunk almost back to where it was before I was pregnant but I couldn't stare at myself any longer. Emotionally this would be a very hard day for me and my flat belly only reminded me that our time together had come to an end.

I twisted the towel around my wet hair and went to my closet to fetch my nicest black pants and a silk blouse. After getting dressed I dried my hair and put on a little makeup. I never wore much but today warranted at least a little blush.

As I pulled into the dedicated parking garage on the other side of town, my phone rang. Herb was already at the courthouse looking for me and I let him know I would be there in five minutes.

"Oh, by the way, the papers were emailed to me this morning," he said, before hanging up. "I'm not sure the court will accept them, but we'll see what happens."

CHAPTER TWENTY-SIX

A wave of nausea rolled through my body. I was in complete shock, Stormie; suddenly everything clicked into place and it all became very real. I was going to court to give up my rights to you, the child that I had sacrificed everything for. I had to tell a judge that I wanted nothing to do with my sweet Stormie, when that couldn't be further from the truth.

The courtroom was large, with rows and rows of dark wooden benches. Two women sat in the back, their hair pulled up neatly, both wearing crisp suits holding file folders on their laps. They were from the hospital legal team and had come to witness the transfer of custody so they could relay the situation to the hospital. Herb sat up front at a large table in front of the first row of benches. A brown-haired woman sat behind him, her hands on his shoulders. *She must be his wife*, I thought.

There were two microphones at the table where Herb sat and another table to the right with the same set-up. In front of them, rising five feet above the ground, stood the judge's desk. The black leather chair behind it was empty but would soon be filled by the judge who would decide our fate together.

I walked down the marble-tiled aisle towards Herb who stood when he saw me.

"This is my wife," he said, motioning to the brunette behind him.

I nodded, shaking her hand.

A guard appeared from a door to the right of the judge's desk and announced her arrival. The entire room stood on their feet while she walked up the steps to her chair and sat down. She was an older woman with thin blonde hair falling in a straight bob to the bottom of her chin. Her robe made her appear large, but I could tell by her skinny fingers and defined cheekbones that she was quite petite.

Herb stood and gave the basic details of the case, then the judge handed me papers to look over. As I held the pen in my hand, my eyes scanning every line, I could feel my heart race. I looked back at the doors to the courtroom to make sure Roger and Ursula hadn't burst through, wanting to claim you as their own. I kept asking myself how I could ever let you go. Rachel and her family were a perfect fit for you but I still couldn't imagine not seeing you every day. However, I knew if I didn't give up my rights to you there was a good chance the Stones would come to Michigan and try to take you from me. They had all the wealth and influence to hire the best lawyers, but I could not subject you to that, no matter how hard it would be to give you up for adoption.

I turned back to the papers before me and flipped to the last page. I had not comprehended anything I had just read and quickly signed my name on the blank line at the bottom, holding back my tears. The guard came and took them from my hands and delivered them to the judge.

The judge quickly looked through the paperwork and found my signature, immediately stating to everyone in the courtroom that I had given up my rights to you and that Mr.. Stone's affidavit would be accepted as well.

Neither Roger nor I would legally have any right to your wellbeing from here on out.

The court was dismissed and Herb and his wife walked me out to my car as tears streamed down my face. His wife handed me a few tissues as we exited the building.

When it was all over I wanted to go back and tell the judge I had changed my mind. I felt as if all that sacrifice meant nothing because I wasn't fighting anymore. I was passing you along to someone else. I had gotten so accustomed to fighting for you that relinquishing that control tore at my heart. To do it, especially with the change in plans that had so suddenly occurred, felt like torture. I had been preparing myself to bring you home, even if only for a short time.

I felt cheated.

I drove back to the hospital after signing the papers in court and spent the next few hours sitting with you alone.

"Please, Stormie, forgive me," I said to you through my tears, over and over again. "I beg you, Stormie, forgive me, Stormie..."

You felt my tension, whining and squirming in my hands. I tried to calm myself down by recounting all the reasons why the choice I had made was the best for all of us.

Your adoptive parents were wonderful and they were much better equipped to handle all the special care you would require as you grew. And I knew they understood the unique bond we shared. Part of me felt like I had just gained a family. Still, as I stared into your eyes, I hoped someday you would find it in your broken heart to forgive me.

Strength does
not come from
physical capacity.
It comes from an
indomitable will.

—Mahatma Gandhi

CHAPTER TWENTY-SEVEN
June 25, 2013

Two pink balloons adorned the mailbox of a big stone
house set back near the woods. A large van was
parked in front of the garage, along with a catering truck.
I pulled my car up alongside the others, where I had parked
the last time we were here. Today was a special day, though, so
I made sure to pull all the way up to the garage door, leaving
plenty of room for other vehicles.

"We're here," I said, just loudly enough for Emmy and
Anne to hear me. Both girls had been asleep in the back almost the
entire way.

"Emmy, wake up! We're here! We're at Stormie's house!"
Emmy stirred, a smile beaming across her face as she rubbed

260

her eyes and yawned. They had both grown up so much in the last year. Anne was getting ready to start Kindergarten and Emmy was speaking in full sentences, desperately trying to keep up with her big sister.

As I unbuckled each of the girls, I reminded them to grab their bags. Emmy and Anne had each made something special for you and I knew they would be left in the car if we didn't bring them in right away. I struggled to grasp the rest of what I had brought, almost falling into the backseat as I reached for the presents we had purchased. We didn't have much in the way of money, but I had managed to get a big birthday balloon, a teddy-bear, and an adorable outfit for you. I hadn't asked Rachel yet, but I was hoping you could wear it for the party.

As I floundered up the steps carrying the gifts and a bag for the girls, I heard the screen door open, and the squealing began. Within seconds Anne and Emmy had stripped off their socks and shoes and were running into the backyard to play with the other children. I put everything down on the love seat next to the door and took a deep breath.

"Hey, Rachel! Where are you?"

The large French doors opened and I could see Rachel walking towards me with you in her arms. You looked adorable, Stormie, with the little bit of hair you had up in a clip and a sunny yellow dress on. As you got closer you smiled when you realized it was me, your entire face lighting up with joy.

"Hey there, you!" Rachel greeted me warmly. "I was just cleaning up. You're early. Come on in!"

"I know. I came early on purpose," I said. "I need some baby time before I have to share her with the rest of the guests. Ya know?"

We laughed. It had been hard to get together the last

SAVING STORMIE: THE BABY S STORY

few times we had tried. You'd had your surgery, and I had been
struggling to balance the girls' new schedules with my own work
calendar and the demands of finding a new place for us to live.
Now that it was summer again, and I was working steadily, we
had been trying to get together more. It was difficult with two
families, especially when doctors' appointments and other limiting
factors got in the way, but recently Rachel had explained to me that
I needn't worry about losing touch with them or feeling as if they
were going to become distant with me. She assured me I would be
in your life forever.

Rachel placed you in my arms and you whirled your head
around to look at me. Your inquisitive nature shone brightly through
your eyes as we looked at one another. I was so proud of the way
you were growing; looking so big and getting so strong. Some
complications you suffered during the first hospitalization period
had limited your mobility, and a few doctors said that you might
not ever walk or talk, or that you might have learning disabilities.
But I could see you better than those who looked at you and only
saw your challenges. You may have been born with a cleft lip and
palette, but that was simply a barrier. Once your heart got better, the
rest would come.

We made our way over to the couch, your legs surprisingly
long as I placed you on my lap. You started to reach for my glasses so
I shifted you over to the other side, so you wouldn't pull them off my
face. As I moved you, your dress slid up and revealed the little button
for your gastrostomy tube on the right side of your body. Because
your anatomy is backwards, your stomach is on your right and your
liver is on your left. Your little heart sits midline, unlike most people
where it is slightly to the left. To look at you, you look much like any
other child, other than a small straight scar going down your chest

and a tube that connects to a pump that feeds you. The exuberance in your eyes and the way you attack everything you go for isn't inhibited by the equipment. Most people don't even know they are there. You act like a normal baby, interested in other people and ready to move.

You tried to wriggle out of my hands as I held you and talked to you, your feet kicking until I placed them on my knees where you could bounce. A smile crossed your face as you continued to bend your legs and launch your body up and down, squealing as you jounced.

Anne and Emmy heard you yell and rushed to come over to see you.

"Stormie!" they shouted in unison. You whipped around, your eyes searching out the source of this new sound. You reached for Emmy's hair, then Anne's, stretching as far as you could.

"Careful," Rachel called. "She's got a thing for hair right now. And Crystal, watch your glasses. She loves mine!"

I laughed as I held you back from pulling out strands of hair from my girls' heads.

There was a lot to do before the other guests arrived, so Rachel and I spent a few hours getting the house cleaned up, weaving around each other as we put out party favors and drinks. I enjoyed spending time with everyone at the house and always felt welcome, even with Rachel's family. There were always six to nine children running around her house but she never faltered, her demeanor remaining quiet and calm. And even though you were a part of an affluent family, their humility made Rachel and her family even more likable.

Soon people started to trickle in. Rachel's sisters, neighbors, and some old friends arrived with their kids. The yard became a giant playground, complete with a wooden play-set, a bounce house, and a plane-shaped see-saw big enough for seven children. A sprinkler set up on the side yard made for a great spot to cool off in the hot June weather. Anne and Emmy were running around with your big sister and a few of the neighbors' boys, dashing through the sprinkler, up the ladder and down the slide. It looked like so much fun and brought me back to times when I was a child.

I pushed Emmy on the swings for a little while until I noticed your father bringing you out of the house. You were passed around the yard while I stood back, watching elated family and friends interact with you.

After you had been outside for a while, Rachel brought out your chair and announced it was time for cake. Your face lit up as the tower of sugar was revealed and placed in front of you. It was a fondant cake, reminiscent of Eric Carle, with little fruits all over the sides and a caterpillar on the top. A smaller cake, just for you, was topped with whipped cream. As it came down to eye level your mouth dropped open and your eyes widened. You reached for it, and almost before you could see the whole thing, you grabbed a handful and shoved it into your mouth. Tasting the sweetness, you went in for another bite, then another, spreading whipped cream all over your face.

We were all snapping pictures and calling out to you when you noticed us standing there. Your focus was so intense that it took a few minutes to get your attention. As soon as you saw the crowd before you, you gave us all the death stare and pulled your cake into your body. I think you thought we were going to take it from you. Emmy was standing by your side and you reached out and pushed her hand off your chair. By the time you were done with your cake it was smashed all over the tray, and your dress was a mess.

Rachel picked you up out of your seat, while you waved

frantically trying to get back to the cake. We brought you inside and you started crying when you realized we were going to strip you down. However, the moment you saw the taps turn on in the sink, your little wail turned to smiles. You put your hands in the water, splashing around while your dad sponged you off. When you were clean, they handed you to me.

"Why don't you go ahead and put her in the birthday outfit you brought her," Rachel said.

I was so excited. I had been hoping I could get some pictures of you in your birthday present. I took you up to your room and got you dressed, then brought you over to the rocking chair in the corner and sat with you. It was nice to have some alone-time, away from everyone at the party.

As you began to close your eyes I reached into the back pocket of my jeans. I had written a letter to you and it felt like the perfect time to read it to you.

Dear Stormie:

It's hard to look back at all you've accomplished this year and not be amazed. You are turning one, but your resilience began long before your birth. From the challenges of being an embryo, created in a petri dish, and frozen for years just waiting for your chance, to the extreme test of survival during the thawing process and implantation, it is hard for anyone to doubt that you do not have an extraordinary will to live.

I still have a hard time coming to terms with the diagnoses you have been handed in life. Some of these are so devastating in clinical presentation and yet you seem to shine on regardless. You have baffled your doctors and shown us all that medical diagnoses are not infallible. Even with a brain deformity that carries about an 85% death rate in early infancy, you are still here, and you are growing and learning more and more every day. You are a miracle baby and I'll tell anyone who asks that I truly believe you will do more than anybody thinks you are capable of.

I didn't enter into surrogacy looking for an existential experience. I just wanted to give someone the chance to be a better person for the sake of a child. It was a transformation I had seen in myself and in others. But you gave me so much more than I could ever have given anyone else. You expanded my heart as much as you expanded my body, creating strength and determination that I never knew I could have. You introduced me to a whole group of people I am so, so thankful to have met, and you showed me that life, no matter how seemingly insignificant, can mean everything to the right people.

I am proud to have kept you safe for the time you were entrusted to me. And yes, I still deal every day with the wish that I could have you by my side as you grow. I see such beauty and joy in your eyes and I wish I could be a much bigger part of that than I am able to be. But I also know that you are absolutely in the best possible hands and that you have a wonderful loving family who will give you everything you need and desire. I hope that everyone can see a little bit of me in you, but even more than that, I hope you can show everyone that just because your life isn't 'normal' it doesn't mean it isn't worth living.

Much like the tree etched on the precious purple journal, we have weathered the storm together and come out stronger, determined to stretch our limbs, revealing the indestructible force within us. All my children have a place on this tree, nestled in the branches where I protected you for so long.

I may not have you with me today, but know that you are forever in my heart. I love you, baby girl. Stay strong and keep proving everyone wrong.

Your Momma

THE END.

CHAPTER TWENTY-SEVEN

A very heartfelt thank you to all of the people who made this journey possible. I love you more than you will ever know. I am so incredibly honored that you were present in my struggle and there to see it come to such a wonderful outcome. Some of you remained in the forefront of my surrogacy venture while others stayed behind the scenes, but every single person who helped me is in some way responsible for ensuring that Stormie and I stayed strong and could see our challenges through to the very end. Without you we would have been lost.

I especially want to thank my mom. No matter what lies in the past, we are bound to one another because we went through this together. I love you!

R and T, thank you for everything you have done for me and Stormie in the past, present, and for the amazing part you play in our future. I can't tell you how glad I am that you are the ones taking care of this sweet girl, holding her in your hearts and helping her grow to her fullest potential. I am a better person for my experience with you.

Made in the USA
Middletown, DE
04 March 2016